# The Southern Harvest

## COOKBOOK

• RECIPES CELEBRATING FOUR SEASONS •

## CATHY CLEARY

*Featuring photography by Katherine Brooks*

AMERICAN PALATE

Published by American Palate
A Division of The History Press
Charleston, SC
www.historypress.net

*Cover images by Katherine Brooks.*

First published 2018

Manufactured in the United States

ISBN 9781467139113

Library of Congress Control Number: 2017955902

THIS BOOK IS DEDICATED TO ANYONE WHO HAS EVER PREPARED
A MEAL FOR SOMEONE ELSE. SHARING FOOD HELPS REMIND US WHO WE ARE,
AND IT'S JUST PLAIN NICE.

# Note

## PROCEEDS TO FOOD SECURITY AND FOOD JUSTICE

Fifty percent of the author's proceeds from this book will support nonprofit organizations working on issues of food justice, sustainable agriculture, food security and edible education initiatives.

*In this time of plenty for some, many people in our communities do not have access to quality food on a daily basis. Children are the hardest hit by this lack of access and have the most to lose in terms of their health and well-being. Children also have the most to gain in terms of edible education. Learning how to grow vegetables and fruits along with basic preparation techniques equips them with skills they can use for the rest of their lives and allows them to shape a world vision of equity for all.*

*I feel passionate about shining a light on this situation and helping to make a difference. There are many nonprofit organizations working to provide more than food to people struggling to maintain a healthy food supply. Providing information about cooking and growing food strengthens communities in a multitude of ways. Not only does higher consumption of fruits and vegetables equal better overall health, but growing, preparing and eating food together builds lasting relationships and fosters trust as well. Edible education and community gardens enable people to have greater control over their food access and security.*

*Food is one of our most basic needs, and fresh, wholesome food should not have to be a luxury. If you have purchased this book, know that your dollars are supporting a vision of health and food access for all people. If you received this book as a gift, please consider purchasing a copy to pass on to someone who might be inspired by it.*

*Find out more by getting in touch with me at my website cathycleary.com or thecookandgarden.com.*

# Contents

# CONTENTS

# CONTENTS

# CONTENTS

# CONTENTS

# Acknowledgements

Reid Chapman, the remarkable person I refer to as "my husband" throughout this book, gave me the concept and the encouragement to embark on this project. It would not have happened without his support.

Elizabeth Woodman, with Eno Publishers, gave me creative input, thoughtful constructive criticism and helpful advice before finally giving me away to another publisher. Her knowledge and experience helped shape this project in directions I never imagined.

It's hard to put into words how much I appreciate Katherine Brooks, the amazing photographer responsible for most of the photos in this book. She put in hours and hours of creative energy to show off the dishes simply and beautifully. Her enthusiasm and support propelled me forward at times when my own enthusiasm was flagging.

My longtime friend and chief recipe tester Katrina Carus tested over seventy-five recipes, giving me detailed write-ups of each one, including hilarious accounts of family members' reactions. Her encouragement and love gave me confidence when my own recipe testing went awry.

In addition to Trina, there were many more friends who tested recipes, including Elizabeth Woodman, Gita Schonfeld, Henry Read, Isaiah Perkinson, Jennifer Thomas,

# ACKNOWLEDGEMENTS

Karen Ostergaard, Kathleen Taylor, Kimberly Masters, Kristin Cozzolino, Nan Kramer, Nancy Robbins, Peggy Myers, Rachel Canada, Rebecca Bodenheimer, Robin Hamilton, Robin Mehler, Scott and Rachel Pohlman, Stephanie Hellert and Valerie Sen. To them I give many thanks for time, effort and energy expended to make recipes easier to follow and more delicious.

Stephanie Hellert and Elizabeth Davis, both dear friends who have much better grammar than I do, helped pre-edit many of my stories. I appreciate them both for making me sound more intelligent than I should take credit for.

My friends Eric and Vanessa Osborne lent me gorgeous pottery and serving dishes as props for many of my photo shoots.

Matt Christie, owner and designer of Green River Woods, lent me some of his beautiful cutting boards to use in photo shoots.

Reba Frady McCracken, mother to my dear friend Gary, shared her tried-and-true southern recipes with me and reminded me that people have been making some of the same delicious dishes for friends and family for generations.

Fellow cookbook author and friend Barbara Swell gave me photography advice and lots of encouragement along the way.

My big sister Peggy Myers inherited the organization gene. She helped me get organized, and I will never stop looking up to her with love and admiration.

Many thanks to my friend and web designer Valerie Leeper for offering sound advice, words of encouragement and endless support.

Longtime friend and collaborator Kimberly Masters has always helped me with projects like this one. I appreciate her skills, ideas and friendship.

The editors and designers at The History Press and Arcadia Publishing were easy to work with, kind and helpful.

Finally, I have to thank all of the chefs who took time away from ever-present kitchen duties to speak with me and tell me their stories. Aaron Vandermark, Andrea Reusing, April McGregor, April Moon Harper, Bill Smith, John Fleer, John Stehling, Karen Taylor, Keith Rhodes and Vivian Howard all had wonderful perspectives and quality cooking advice to share. It was a pleasure getting to know them a bit better.

# Introduction

Apparently, I'm not normal. Most folks get excited about hot doughnuts or a platter of apple wood–smoked barbecue. My mouth waters at the sight of a basket full of sunny-colored summer squash. I start imagining how it would taste seared and layered with goat cheese or marinated along with fresh herbs, lemon and garlic. Images of pickles and stuffed squash blossoms tease me, and I have to take that basket from the garden into the kitchen to get started.

Often the fruits and vegetables put themselves together according to what ripens at the same time. Asparagus, strawberries and violets, all ready to pick, look and taste beautiful together. Figs, hazelnuts and multicolored sweet peppers all appear in market stalls along with the first crisp mornings of fall. It seems obvious they are meant to be consumed on the same plate. Inspiration is not far away when produce is so obliging.

The year we grew a field of dent corn is a particularly good example. I had no idea one small plot could yield so much food. It didn't look like much in October as we harvested the corn cobs drying on the stalks. I consulted farmer friends and was advised to continue the drying process in the barn for another month before beginning to grind kernels into cornmeal and grits. Dusting off a hand-cranked grain grinder, I laboriously shelled my first cob, ground it up, sifted out the chaff and could hardly believe I had over a cup of cornmeal and enough grits to feed two hungry breakfast eaters—not only that, but the flavor was better than any I'd ever experienced. The mouthwatering visions of fresh chilies mixed into cheese grits and zucchini-flecked Asiago corn muffins began.

That winter, I invited friends, neighbors and hungry teenagers over for corn parties. I borrowed an antique corn sheller attached to a bench and let the kids have all the fun, turning the crank and watching the kernels fall off cobs into the box below. We got great arm workouts grinding up all the corn by hand and sifting it through my makeshift sieves. I made cheesy hot polenta with the fresh cornmeal, and everyone left with a bag of grits to cook up at home.

All told, we yielded at least one hundred pounds of grain, feeding ourselves and many other mouths. Our little field of dent corn gave rise to loads of laughter, a kitchen covered in corn kernels, grits soufflé and sweet potato cornbread.

Using up every bit of that corn and conserving resources by sharing equipment, labor and ultimately food are just as inspiring to me as the produce itself.

In a society where food waste is at an all-time high, I want to find ways to preserve, cook, share and consume the food I purchase or grow. That means getting creative when bumper crops of collards and sweet potatoes come in or baskets of peaches and apples overflow the market. Pickled collard greens, sweet potato chocolate ginger pie, bourbon basil peach preserves and apple coleslaws were all born from the desire to ensure nothing be wasted.

Growing up in the South and cooking with seasonal produce, I draw heavily on southern culinary traditions, and frugal southern cooks had many lessons to share. Using bones for homemade stock is becoming popular again, and collard greens cooked with the Christmas ham bone isn't just trendy, it's thrifty. Green tomatoes aren't just tomatoes that will never be ripe before first frost. Most folks know they are great fried; they're also excellent pickled or paired with sweet crisp apples in a salad. Drawing on and playing with these lessons of thrift means when green beans fill all my available baskets, I dream up green bean fritters with falafel spices.

Exploring the historical connection between southern culinary traditions and enslaved African cooks—a crucial link that is so obvious and so often ignored—is also inspirational and brings a whole new dimension to Carolina red rice. Grits with shrimp and greens on top look very similar to dishes I saw traveling in West Africa, and chili garlic sauce reminds me of the shito sauces I made while cooking in a Ghanaian kitchen. Paying homage to the cooks who brought their traditions with them through a horrible journey to an alien world reminds me that food helps transcend pain, bringing comfort as well as sustenance.

There are so many lessons to be learned and so much love to be shared through the food we prepare. Whether I am working in a kitchen with a seasoned chef or an eight-year-old cutting zucchini to make pickles, I learn new ways to make a sauce or cut a vegetable. My sincerest hope is for people to enjoy vegetables as much as I do, and sharing my inspirations and lessons learned might mean that more folks leave jars of pickled collard greens on other people's porches.

# · S P R I N G ·

# 1

## Spring Greens

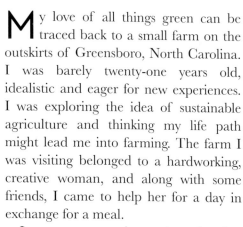

My love of all things green can be traced back to a small farm on the outskirts of Greensboro, North Carolina. I was barely twenty-one years old, idealistic and eager for new experiences. I was exploring the idea of sustainable agriculture and thinking my life path might lead me into farming. The farm I was visiting belonged to a hardworking, creative woman, and along with some friends, I came to help her for a day in exchange for a meal.

It was a sunny, crisp, early spring day, and the farmer gave us the task of double digging some new garden beds. It was hard, hungry-making work, and when we stopped for lunch, I was looking forward to a hearty meal. Everything we ate for lunch came from the farm, including the freshly picked arugula salad. I watched as garlic was rubbed in a big wooden salad bowl; then vinegar, oil, salt and pepper were added. Tender crisp greens got tossed with the vinaigrette for a simple side dish. My first bite of that salad was also my first ever taste of arugula, and the slightly spicy, nutty flavor was the beginning of a love affair.

I could not get enough of that salad and began to search out arugula, which was not ubiquitous at the time. As I explored this new world of flavor, I discovered many other varieties of greens that were more complex in texture and taste than I had ever imagined. I did not end up pursuing farming right away, but I did end up with a vegetable patch at every house I've ever lived since that day on the farm. If all I can grow is a little bit of arugula and maybe some kale or mustard greens, I know I will eat well.

After over a decade of owning a bakery, people are often surprised when I tell them my favorite food is salad. To be clear, the bakery was also a café, and we always featured tasty salads. I thought folks might come for the sweets but stay for the salads, and in fact, some claimed they did. If I had to state a mission in this life, it would be sharing that same sense of vegetable-loving wonder I felt when tasting arugula for the first time.

# Strawberry Pea Shoot Salad

### SERVES 4

In the chill of winter, I tromp out to the garden to uncover thick, hearty kale, collard and chard leaves and cut them into small bits for my winter salads. I love my winter salads, laced with roasted root vegetables and chopped apples, but as the tender lettuces and pea shoots start to emerge in spring, I'm overjoyed. I know the neighbors think I'm crazy as they watch me graze on pea shoots in the yard, but did I mention salad is my favorite food?

## SALAD INGREDIENTS

8 cups (5 ounces) pea shoots,
   or any spring salad green
I cup sliced strawberries
½ cup blanched asparagus spears
¼ cup cooked bacon, crumbled

¼ cup violets (optional)
½ cup toasted nuts (optional)
¼ cup crumbled goat cheese (optional)
⅓ cup strawberry vinaigrette or bottled
   balsamic vinaigrette

### Strawberry Vinaigrette

½ cup (4 large) whole strawberries
½ cup cider vinegar
½ cup extra virgin or light olive oil
1 clove garlic, crushed and peeled

1–2 Tablespoons sugar
½ teaspoon salt
¼ teaspoon vanilla extract

*Chop pea shoots into bite-sized pieces and layer in a salad bowl with remaining salad ingredients. Blend together all vinaigrette ingredients in a blender or food processor. Drizzle salad with ⅓ cup of the vinaigrette just before serving or serve with dressing on the side. Reserve extra dressing for future salads, or use as a marinade for asparagus or other spring veggies. Will keep for two weeks in the fridge. Serve alongside Herb Focaccia, a mushroom omelet, Ramp and Ricotta Biscuits, roasted fish or grilled chicken.*

# Deviled Egg Asparagus Salad

### SERVES 8

At every Easter brunch I've ever attended (and growing up Catholic I've been to a lot), there was asparagus in some form and deviled eggs. I've always thought eggs and asparagus tasted delicious together, and this salad means my nephew can't eat half of the deviled eggs before anyone else gets to them.

*Author photo.*

## DEVILED EGGS

10 eggs
¼ cup mayonnaise
2 Tablespoons softened butter
2 Tablespoons chopped fresh herbs
  (parsley, thyme or dill)

½ teaspoon salt
½ teaspoon sugar
½ teaspoon Dijon mustard
½ teaspoon fresh ground pepper
  or paprika

## DRESSING

¼ cup deviled egg filling
¼ cup mayonnaise
2 Tablespoons cider vinegar
2 Tablespoons water
1 Tablespoon sugar
½ teaspoon salt

## SALAD BASE

1 bunch (about 18 spears) asparagus
8 cups (5 ounces) salad greens
1 cup roasted beets or grated carrots

> ### STEAMING FRESH EGGS
>
> If an egg is very fresh when boiled, it can often be difficult to peel. When you want to make beautiful deviled eggs, it's frustrating to have half of the white come off as you peel them. Steaming the eggs works much better. Place a steamer basket in a wide-bottomed sauce pot. Put about an inch of water in the pot—make sure the water level is below the basket. Bring the water to a boil, turn heat to low and then carefully place your eggs in a single layer in the basket. Simmer covered for fifteen minutes. Turn off the heat and leave covered five more minutes. Run cold water into the pot to cover the eggs and stop cooking.

*Hard cook eggs by boiling or steaming. Peel eggs and slice in half lengthwise. Remove yolks and combine in a bowl with mayonnaise, butter, herbs, salt, sugar, mustard and pepper. Mash yolk mixture with a fork and mix well. Set aside ¼ cup for salad dressing.*

*Slice egg whites lengthwise again so that each half becomes a quarter. Put about ½ teaspoon of yolk mixture on top of each egg white quarter. Make dressing by whisking together ingredients.*

*Prepare asparagus by trimming off tough ends and cutting into bite-sized lengths. (Optional: sauté in a hot skillet with 1 teaspoon oil and ¼ teaspoon salt for 2–3 minutes until asparagus is bright green. Allow to cool.) In a large bowl, layer greens, beets or carrots and asparagus. Decorate top of the salad with deviled eggs. Serve with dressing on the side. Offer as a special brunch salad with ham, Sweet Potato Biscuits and chili cheese grits.*

## Shrimp Grits and Greens

SERVES 4

My mother-in-law insists that shrimp are easier to peel after they have been cooked, and my husband says the opposite. This is pretty typical for their relationship. I personally am staying silent on the subject, which is also typical when it comes to participating in their disputes. However, I will say cooking shrimp in their shells makes them taste better. A quick reheat in the delicious buttery shrimp broth is all they need.

### GRITS

4 cups water
1 cup yellow corn grits
   (not quick or instant)
1 cup grated sharp Cheddar
2 ounces cream cheese
1 teaspoon salt

### SHRIMP

2 cheap beers, pilsner or brown ale
   (not IPA)
1 teaspoon salt
¾–1 pound shrimp, unpeeled
3 Tablespoons butter
2 cloves garlic, very finely diced
Hot sauce to taste

### GREENS

2 teaspoons extra virgin olive oil
8–10 cups (1 pound) Swiss chard,
   spinach, young kale or sweet potato
   greens
2 cloves garlic, very finely diced
¼ teaspoon salt

### HARVESTING AND WASHING GREENS

I grow copious amounts of greens. Little patches of greens are scattered all over my yard year round. They are hearty and vigorous, requiring little of me until I harvest them. Honestly, I feel they are easier to grow than to wash. Grit, dirt and bugs love to cling to the undersides of those nutritious leaves. Over the years, I have come up with a method for washing that seems pretty effective. Harvest greens into a two- or three-gallon tub or bucket, fill with water so that greens are submerged, allow to soak for two to five minutes, then scoop handfuls of greens out of the water into a salad spinner. For extra gritty greens remove spinner basket from bowl and rinse greens under fresh cool water before spinning in salad spinner to remove as much water as possible. Taste a leaf or two to make sure the grit is gone. Repeat the process if necessary.

Capture that wash water and put it back on your plants!

In a heavy-bottomed sauce pan, bring the water to a boil. Pour in grits while stirring, gradually, so that no lumps form. Turn heat to medium low; stir in cheeses and salt. Cook the grits 30 minutes, stirring every 5–10 minutes. While grits are cooking, start working on the shrimp. Bring the beer and salt to a boil in a sauce pot. Add the unpeeled shrimp and bring back to a boil. Remove immediately from the heat. Shrimp should be pink but not cooked completely. Reserve about 2 cups of the cooking liquid and drain the rest off of the shrimp. Peel the shrimp, cut them in half lengthwise and remove veins. (This is a great thing to have a helper with!)

Heat oil in a skillet over medium heat and add the greens, garlic and salt. Stir just until greens are wilted.

Just before serving, reheat the shrimp cooking liquid in the pot and add the butter, garlic and hot sauce to taste. Bring this to a boil, add the shrimp and remove from heat (thus not overcooking the shrimp).

Serve the grits in bowls with greens, shrimp and a little of the cooking liquid on top if desired.

# Lemony Garlic Greens with Shrimp and Pasta

### SERVES 4

There is a fish shack on the side of the road close to where my in-laws live, and whenever we visit, we stop in to get a big bag of shrimp. I chat with the owners about which boat came in that day and always end up getting more fish than planned because it is so fresh. Fortunately, shrimp freezes beautifully, and I can make this dish any time of year. In summer, I use sweet potato leaves; spring time, pea shoots; fall, spinach; and winter, kale. If you chat your way into too much shrimp, I highly recommend this garlicky green remedy.

¾ pound fettuccine, spaghetti or penne pasta

1 lemon, finely grated zest, and juice

4 cloves garlic, finely diced or crushed

1¼ teaspoons salt

2 teaspoons extra virgin olive oil

¾–1 pound of shrimp, peeled and deveined

8–10 cups (1 pound) chopped kale, spinach, Swiss chard, sweet potato leaves, or pea shoots

¾ cup freshly grated Parmesan cheese

Bring about 8 cups of water to a boil in a large pot. Add pasta and simmer, covered, for about 8 minutes. Pasta will be al dente. Reserve 1 cup cooking water and drain remaining water from pasta.

In the pot, combine reserved water, pasta, lemon zest and juice, garlic, salt and olive oil. Simmer on low heat, stirring occasionally, for 2–3 minutes. Taste pasta, and if you want it softer, cook a bit longer.

Add shrimp, greens and cheese to the pot and cook, stirring several minutes until shrimp are nice and pink and greens are wilted. Remove from heat and serve immediately, with Herb Focaccia and Cucumber Cherry Tomato Salad or Roasted Root Vegetables and Arugula Apple Salad in winter.

## Greens and Eggs

SERVES 3–4

This is a good second breakfast or casual brunch alongside potatoes or cheese grits. I'm an early riser and like a bite of something on the sweet side first thing. I'll eat a little granola or maybe some yogurt and fruit, but then about 11:00 a.m., I am really ready for something delicious and savory. This is quick and easy—not to mention pretty.

*Author photo.*

1 Tablespoon extra virgin olive oil or
   bacon grease
½ cup red or yellow onion, diced
¼ cup red pepper, diced (optional)
½ teaspoon salt
8–10 cups (1 pound) chopped spinach,
   kale, Swiss chard, baby bok choy, turnip,
   mustard or sweet potato greens

1 teaspoon cider vinegar or water
3–4 eggs
Fresh black pepper and salt
   for sprinkling

*In a 9- or 10-inch skillet, heat the oil on medium-high heat. Sauté onion, pepper and salt 2–3 minutes. Add the greens and vinegar and sauté until greens start to wilt—30 seconds to 5 minutes depending on your greens. Make 3–4 holes in the greens so that you can see the bottom of the pan.*

*Crack eggs in the holes; sprinkle with a little salt and pepper. Cover the skillet, and turn the heat to low. Cook for about 5 minutes, until eggs are desired doneness. Using a spatula, scoop out sunny side up eggs onto plates and arrange greens around them. Serve with roasted veggies, baked potatoes or Ricotta Grits Soufflé.*

# 2

## Spring Perennials

Perennial plants die back in autumn, but in springtime, they return year after year without needing to be re-seeded. Think berry bushes, mint, daffodils and fruit trees. In tropical climates, there are loads of perennials; for instance, tomato vines can live on and on if never exposed to cold.

Our climate allows for lots of perennial fruits, flowers and herbs, but not as many vegetables. Three of my personal favorites from this short list are asparagus, ramps and rhubarb. I eagerly anticipate the first tender shoots of asparagus that poke through the warming spring soil in my yard. They come when the time is right; gardeners cannot schedule their arrival. As a rather lazy gardener, I greatly appreciate not needing to micromanage my asparagus. Ramps and rhubarb operate similarly, waiting until the ground is warm and moist enough with spring rains to unfurl their first green leaves.

Cherry trees loaded with pink blooms in early spring are also some of the first fruit I get to pick in my yard. I remember the year I was out of town for the same exact two weeks the cherries were ripe, I had to be satisfied with friends' pictures of their kids picking cherries off my tree. Fortunately, Chef Aaron Vandermark shared his recipe for pickled cherries so I can enjoy them many more weeks of the year.

Ultimately, perennials make me happy because they remind me I am not in charge. Some things can take care of themselves, and with just a little bit of love (and mulch), they give back much in return.

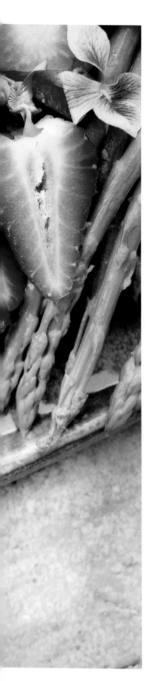

# Asparagus with Strawberries and Violets

### SERVES 4-6

We have an asparagus patch in the yard, and in early spring, delicate green spears begin to poke out of the ground like magic. Strawberries and violets appear just like the asparagus, seemingly unbidden. Perennial plants that come back every year are my favorites. They are like a surprise gift I'm happy to see but didn't expect. The hard part is waiting to gobble them up until I can gather enough to make this delicious dish.

## STRAWBERRY MARINADE

½ cup (4 large) whole strawberries
½ cup cider vinegar
½ cup extra virgin or light olive oil

I clove garlic, crushed and peeled
1–2 Tablespoons sugar
½ teaspoon salt
¼ teaspoon vanilla extract

## THE DISH

I bunch (20 or so) asparagus spears

I cup sliced strawberries
¼ cup violets or other edible flower

*Blend marinade ingredients in a blender, food processor or food mill. Bring about 2 inches of water to a boil in a nice wide pan. It should be large enough so that the asparagus won't have to bunch or curl to fit in. Add asparagus, and cook for 2–3 minutes until asparagus is bright green. Remove from heat and drain. Toss warm asparagus with ½ cup marinade and let marinate for a few minutes. Remove asparagus to a platter and sprinkle strawberries and flowers on top. Serve warm or at room temperature with remaining marinade on the side for extra drizzling. Pair with Rhubarb Ginger Mostarda with Goat Cheese, garlicky chicken, Ricotta Grits Soufflé or a rainbow chard frittata.*

# Ramp and Ricotta Biscuits

## MAKES 8 BISCUITS

Our patch of ramps was planted by our neighbor a zillion years ago. It's in a shady area near the wood-fired pizza oven I built, and the proximity could not be better. In our part of the country, people have been eating ramps in the springtime for many a generation. Festivals celebrate their arrival and delicious addition to the blandness of winter. Later in spring, ramp flavors become stronger, and copious consumers can experience potent garlicky body odor. That should never ever be a reason to shy away from a ramp in my opinion. The memory of the flavor is well worth an hour or so of garlic-scented skin.

4 Tablespoons cold butter, cut into chunks
1 cup all-purpose flour
½ cup (1 ounce) coarsely chopped ramps, greens and white part
1 teaspoon baking powder
¼ teaspoon baking soda
¼ teaspoon salt
½ cup part skim ricotta cheese
2 Tablespoons milk, soy milk or cream

*Preheat oven to 375 degrees. In a food processor, combine butter and flour; process until the butter is fully incorporated. Add ramps, baking powder, soda and salt. Pulse food processor to chop ramps and incorporate, but do not over process. In a mixing bowl, combine cheese and milk; fold in dry ingredients until just combined.*

*Pat out dough to about 1-inch thickness on a floured surface, and cut out 2-inch biscuits. Gather scraps of dough and pat together to cut out more biscuits. Makes about 8. Put biscuits on a lightly greased sheet pan or parchment-lined pan and bake for 20–25 minutes, until browning on edges.*

*Serve with crème fraiche, goat cheese or butter. These are great alongside smoked pork, asparagus and Strawberry Pea Shoot Salad.*

### SUSTAINABLY HARVESTED RAMPS

I just want to advocate for sustainably harvested ramps. My understanding is that you should never pull out the roots of the ramp plant, and by the same token, you should not buy ramps with roots on. Ramps have become incredibly popular, and this wild crop has been decimated in some areas. In order for plants to grow back the following season, the roots need to be left in the ground. This can be done by digging down and cutting plants just above the roots. If you happen to dig up the roots, cut them off and replant them immediately.

# Rhubarb Ginger Mostarda with Goat Cheese

### MAKES 2 CUPS

*Author photo.*

Our farm came with old rhubarb plants needing to be thinned, so we separated some roots and planted them near our house. When folks walk past, they sometimes think it is ruby red chard, and I have to caution them not to eat the leaves. The leaves are toxic, but the prolific reddish-gold stalks are edible and tasty. When I owned the bakery, springtime meant rhubarb pies, muffins, breads and cobblers. Rhubarb's tart flavor is usually matched with loads of sugar, but I lean toward more savory applications for this beautiful vegetable. There is just enough sugar in this recipe to balance the tartness and make it pair perfectly with cheeses, meats and other vegetables.

## MOSTARDA

½ cup sugar

I small lemon, sliced

¼ cup cider vinegar

2 Tablespoons water

2–3 Tablespoons fresh ginger, peeled and finely diced

2 star anise pods or I cinnamon stick

I teaspoon mustard seeds

½ teaspoon salt

2 cups diced rhubarb stalks

## FOR SERVING

4–6 ounces plain goat cheese, or any kind of cheese, actually
Crackers or bread

*Combine all ingredients except rhubarb in a sauce pot and bring to a boil. Add rhubarb and cook for 2–3 minutes. Turn off the heat and steep for at least 30 minutes. Remove star anise, squeeze and remove lemon and mash rhubarb with a fork. Serve on top of goat cheese and crackers or on grilled pork, alongside salads, on top of vanilla yogurt or ice cream or on open-faced cheese sandwiches. Makes 2 cups. Will keep in the fridge for several weeks.*

# INTERVIEW WITH
# CHEF AARON VANDERMARK

CHEF AND OWNER OF PANCIUTO RESTAURANT IN HILLSBOROUGH, NORTH CAROLINA,
SHARES HIS THOUGHTS ON FOOD AND COOKING

*My childhood food memories swirl in bowls of instant ramen, microwaved hot dogs and Sundays at Golden Corral. I was never going to be a chef. It never once entered my mind. I'm not even sure why I got my first restaurant job. It was probably a poorly conceived plan to get free food. All I know is I spent the summer refilling ice for the bartender, plating prepackaged desserts, opening Coronas on the patio and wearing out that employee discount. It sounds really lame now, but I loved it then. It was physically and mentally draining, a structured riot, an orchestrated chaos. It pushed my buttons, and seventeen years later, I'm still with it.*

*Time and place certainly inform my cooking, and the South provides guidance for creativity. I'm not adhering to, or preserving, southern culinary tradition as much as incorporating its tenets into my creative process. As the South continues to change, so, too, will its culinary future, only to be redefined again and again. While not with overt intention, I suppose we're all contributing to that future.*

*Whether it's July's okra planted by our shed or the restaurant's overwhelming supply of peppers in September, there always comes a time when we have more than we know how to use. There's canning, fermenting, pickling, pesto, juices and freezing, but at the restaurant, we've recently been exploring dehydration, not just as a preservation method but for what it unlocks creatively. For example, drying turnip tops, powdering them with a pinch of salt and using them to season the lightly roasted and buttered turnip roots has been a really fun way to eat a whole turnip. There's a lot to play with here.*

*I make it a point to support environmentally responsible and "quality of life"–conscious farmers in my area. Seeing this in practice while I was coming up in great kitchens set the tone for the way I wanted to work. You've heard it before. The quality of your product is everything, so start there. Ultimately, there's not really much improving on a perfectly ripe peach or any other fruit or vegetable. Its flavor can be enhanced with a pinch of salt, pinch of sugar, drop of vinegar or scratch of ginger, but it's only as good as the peach and the farmer who grew it.*

# Aaron's Pickled Cherries

Our cherries come from my neighbors, Betty and Jerry Eidenier. It's not hyperbole when I say that they're the best in North Carolina, and I'm referring to both the cherries and my neighbors. They're kind enough to share a few bags of these precious gems with us each June, and I feel a responsibility to use them well. Here's one way we extend their presence on the menu at Panciuto.

| | |
|---|---|
| 1 quart sour cherries, pitted | 2 sliced lemon rounds |
| 4 sticks cinnamon | 3 cups red wine vinegar |
| 2 Tablespoons peppercorns | 2 cups sugar |
| 8 cloves | 1 cup water |
| 2 Tablespoons whole allspice berries | |

*Put the cherries into a jar or other container. Crack the cinnamon sticks, rough crush the peppercorns, leave the cloves whole, smash the allspice berries. Combine these spices with everything else in a pot. Boil to simmer for 5 minutes. Remove from heat and let cool on the counter for 10–15 minutes. Pour this over the cherries. Cover and chill. Try not to eat these for 2 weeks, but they get even better with more time. We've used these with everything from ice cream to grilled quail with rousing success.*

# 3

## *Herbs*

Herbs are often the gateway to gardening. Kitchen windows can usually accommodate a pot or two of spindly basil plants or little rosemary topiaries. I recall a dorm room tarragon plant that was much mistreated but managed to survive my freshman year with quite a bit more grace than I could muster.

After moving off campus and into my first apartment, there was more room for an even larger pot of sage, which eventually got planted in the backyard of a co-op house where I lived my senior year. In that yard, my sage joined some rosemary and oregano that friends found in a dumpster behind a garden center (the things people throw away!).

It makes sense to grow your own herbs. Often they are perennial plants that come back year after year, many do well in pots, they are easy to preserve and—most importantly—recipes usually call for small amounts of herbs. I wonder how many thousands of pounds of herbs waste away each year in people's refrigerators because they had to buy an entire bunch of cilantro at the grocery store but only used the two teaspoons called for in a recipe.

I try to stay away from preaching, generally, but I cannot help but recommend growing fresh herbs if you have a window where you live. You don't even need a pot; a plastic cup with a hole in the bottom should do the trick. Seeds are cheap, and cuttings rooted out from a friend are usually free.

The bright, fresh flavors herbs bring to recipes cannot be duplicated any other way. It is hard to imagine making a sauce, soup or salad without a bit of parsley, basil or rosemary. Dried is good, fresh is even better and when they're growing right on your windowsill, you always have what you need for the next recipe.

## *Garlic Herb Cream Cheese*

At our bakery, we made a version of this super easy spread for our bagels. I never ate it on bagels. I stirred it into my tomato soup, spread it on my egg sandwiches, scooped it up with tortilla chips, added it to my breakfast bowl with roasted potatoes and grits or made a little plate of cucumber slices and veggie sticks for dipping. This spread is such a simple thing, yet it makes other things taste extraordinary.

8 ounces cream cheese
2 cloves garlic, minced
1 Tablespoon chopped parsley
   or basil leaves

2 teaspoons chopped rosemary leaves
1 teaspoon thyme leaves (½ teaspoon dried)
¼ teaspoon salt
1 Tablespoon water

*Pull cream cheese from the fridge 2–3 hours before mixing for easier incorporation. Combine all ingredients in the bowl of a stand mixer or mix by hand with a very sturdy spoon. Mix until water is fully incorporated into cream cheese and no more lumps of cheese remain. Serve as a vegetable dip; on pasta, crackers or toast; as a grilled cheese sandwich with spinach; on top of grits or baked potatoes; or stirred into soups.*

# Herb Focaccia

I often encounter folks who are intimidated by yeast breads. Maybe they don't have the right equipment, or maybe they don't know how to knead dough. This is the perfect yeast bread novice recipe. It really is simple, and you don't need fancy equipment or technique. Stir with a spoon if you like. No kneading or shaping necessary. If you can make a clay pancake you can make this bread, and it is much tastier. Use whatever herbs you like. My friend Trina even used hyssop and won rave reviews.

2 cups warm water
2 cups whole wheat flour
1¾ cups all-purpose or bread flour
1 cup mixed fresh herbs, loosely packed, chopped (sage, parsley, basil, rosemary, thyme, oregano, fennel fronds, dill and so on)
1 Tablespoon (1 package) instant yeast

1 Tablespoon sugar
1 Tablespoon salt
1 Tablespoon light olive oil or vegetable oil
1½ teaspoons garlic powder or minced fresh garlic
Extra herbs for garnish (optional)

*In a stand mixer with the paddle attachment (or in a large bowl with a wooden spoon), combine all ingredients except the herbs for garnish. Mix until well combined and then mix or stir on low for about 5 minutes. Dough will be a very wet consistency. Allow to rise, covered, 1 hour.*

*Grease a sheet pan with about 1 Tablespoon olive oil, scrape dough onto sheet pan and, with greased hands, pat out to an approximate 12- by 8-inch rectangle. (It does not have to touch the edges of the pan.) Spread another Tablespoon of oil on top of the dough and sprinkle with a few more fresh herbs if you have them. Allow to rise 1 hour in the pan uncovered.*

*Preheat oven to 425 degrees. Just before baking, use your fingers to make dimple indentions in the top of the dough. Bake for about 20 minutes and allow to cool for a few minutes on the pan. Use a spatula to loosen edges and remove from pan. Slice and serve as an appetizer topped with Garlic Herb Cream Cheese, pesto, hummus or goat cheese or serve alongside soups and salads. Cut in half horizontally and use to make sandwiches.*

# Pestos

People have been combining fragrant leaves with salt, fat and pungent roots like garlic to produce flavorful sauces for eons. Every culture all over the world has some version of this formula. These sauces get rubbed on meat, tossed with grains, spread on breads and drizzled on vegetables. I like to think I'm carrying on an ancient tradition when I make pesto, and just like my ancestors would have used whatever they had on hand, I vary the ingredients wildly. Try incorporating other varieties of herbs, nuts, oils or cheeses to make your pesto your own. Each of the following recipes makes 1 to 1½ cups.

## CREAMY HAZELNUT PESTO

½ cup hazelnuts
4 cups packed herb leaves (parsley, basil, cilantro)
⅓ cup hazelnut oil or extra virgin olive oil

½ cup grated Parmesan cheese
2 ounces cream cheese
1 teaspoon salt
1–2 cloves garlic, crushed and peeled

*Most hazelnuts are not sold toasted, and this is an important step that dramatically changes the flavor of the pesto. To toast nuts, bake them in an oven or toaster oven at 350 degrees for 15–20 minutes. Let nuts cool and then rub them with a towel to remove most of the skins. If using basil leaves, blanch leaves in boiling water and shock in ice water to prevent pesto from browning. Combine all ingredients in a food processor or use a mortar and pestle and process until smooth.*

## LEMON ZEST PESTO

3 cloves garlic, crushed and peeled
1 lemon, finely grated zest and juice
4 cups packed herb leaves (parsley, lemon basil, cilantro)

½ cup grated Parmesan cheese
¼ cup toasted almonds
¼ cup extra virgin olive oil or almond oil
1 teaspoon salt

*Combine garlic and lemon in a food processor or mortar and pestle and process until garlic is chopped. Add remaining ingredients and process until smooth. Substitute 1–2 cups of lemon balm for other herbs if you have it.*

## TOASTED SUNFLOWER CHEDDAR SAGE PESTO

3½ cups packed herb leaves
  (parsley, basil, cilantro)
½ cup sage leaves
1 cup grated Cheddar

½ cup sunflower seeds, toasted
4 Tablespoons butter or olive oil
1–2 cloves garlic, crushed and peeled
1 teaspoon salt

*Combine ingredients in a food processor or mortar and pestle and process until smooth.*

## PRIMARY HERBS TO USE FOR PESTO

4 cups packed = 4 ounces

Parsley
Basil
Cilantro

## SUBSTITUTE SMALL AMOUNTS OF THESE HERBS FOR ADDED FLAVOR

Mint, I cup
Fennel fronds, I cup
Chives, ½ cup
Dill, ½ cup
Sage, ½ cup
Lemon balm, ½ cup
Thyme, ¼ cup
Oregano, ¼ cup
Tarragon, ¼ cup
Sorrel, ¼ cup
Rosemary, ¼ cup

---

### THINK OUTSIDE THE PASTA BOX

Pesto transforms a grilled cheese sandwich and makes an ordinary chicken salad exceptional. These sauces use up the herbs going limp in the fridge and freeze well for a quick appetizer plate with crackers and cut up veggies. Thin pesto down with water or olive oil and dip shrimp in it or call it salad dressing. Spread it on a tortilla, add a bit of cheese and grill. Add some into biscuit dough. Drizzle on beans, grits, soups, roasted veggies, meats, rice or tomato slices.

---

## SUBSTITUTE 1½–2 CUPS GREENS FOR HERBS

Swiss chard, spinach, baby kale, young turnip greens, arugula and pea shoots work well. Chickweed and lambs quarters also work if you want to go wild.

# Homegrown Herb Vinaigrette

Salad dressing might seem like a strange Christmas gift, but I take inspiration wherever I can get it, and one year my bumper crop of parsley inspired the gift of Homegrown Herb Vinaigrette. In early November, as I stood in my garden wondering what the heck I was going to make for Christmas presents, bushy parsley plants waved at me. The green leaves stayed healthy through the first few frosts, and in mid-December, I made huge batches of this dressing. As everyone else was gorging on cookies, my friends and family were happily munching on deliciously dressed lettuce leaves. Makes about ¾ cup.

¼ cup olive oil
¼ cup cider vinegar
2 cloves garlic, crushed and peeled
1 cup packed leafy herbs, such as parsley,
   basil or cilantro

1 Tablespoon sugar
1 teaspoon salt
1 teaspoon Dijon mustard

*Combine ingredients in a blender or food processor and blend until herbs are finely chopped.*

## PRESERVING HERBS

Some herbs take to drying, and others do better in the freezer. In either case, use them within 6–8 months to enjoy the best flavor.

HERBS THAT DRY WELL: parsley, thyme, oregano, sage, lavender, chives, marjoram, chervil and cilantro

HERBS THAT FREEZE WELL: rosemary, fennel seed, coriander seed and bay leaves

There are several methods you can use for drying, depending on the amount of time and equipment you have. Any of the following methods work well. Use freshly picked, cleaned and stemmed herbs. Store dried herbs in clean jars, containers or plastic bags away from heat or light. See page 44 for more methods.

MICROWAVE: Place herbs in a single layer on a paper towel in the microwave and cook for 2 ½–4 minutes depending on the power of your microwave. Herbs should be dry to the touch and crumble easily.

OVEN: Heat your oven to 200 degrees. Place herbs in a single layer on a sheet pan lined with parchment or paper towels. After 10 minutes, turn the oven off and leave herbs in cooling oven for an additional 15–25 minutes. Herbs should be dry to the touch and crumble easily.

ELECTRIC DEHYDRATOR: Place herbs in your dehydrator and dry for 3–5 hours. Herbs should be dry to the touch and crumble easily.

OUTSIDE IN THE SUN: Place herbs on paper towels or newspaper on top of screens or chicken wire in a sunny spot off the ground and away from critters for 4–8 hours. Weigh down the paper with small stones in case it gets breezy. Herbs should be dry to the touch and crumble easily.

HUNG UP BY THE STEMS: Cut whole branches of herbs and secure in bunches with twine or rubber bands. Hang upside down in a sunny window or shed 1–2 weeks. Herbs should be dry to the touch and crumble easily.

To freeze herbs, simply clean and stem them and put them in plastic bags. Label with the date and stick them in the freezer.

## INTERVIEW WITH CHEF BILL SMITH

"Nothing is set in stone; be observant and flexible." Bill Smith, the chef at Crook's Corner in Chapel Hill for over twenty years, could be talking about any type of adventure, but in this case, he is talking about his adventures with food and cooking. He credits this outlook to his mentor, Bill Neil, who gave him his first job as a prep cook peeling potatoes and chopping parsley at La Residence.

All those who have enjoyed Bill's cooking over the years have gone on his adventures with him. His family hails from eastern North Carolina, where he grew up eating his grandmother's collard greens and fried chicken. A lot of his dishes reflect those roots, and here, too, it was the attitude he learned that impacted him the most. "My grandmother had the expectation that every time you sat down the food should be a) good and b) fun." It was an invaluable lesson that Bill took to heart.

That sense of fun and adventure keeps him open to new possibilities. Years ago, a woman named Mrs. Andrews called him out of the blue saying, "I've got mint in my flower bed and I'll sell you one hundred stems for six dollars." After buying her mint, Bill discovered she also had figs, persimmons, pecans and Jerusalem artichokes. She and her neighbors, all home gardeners, have supplied him with hard-to-find ingredients for more than twenty years.

Bill's enthusiasm is apparent as he describes his inspirations: "A new season revs you up, with new ingredients to work with. I'm delighted to see tomatoes and soft shell crabs." He also credits his fellow cooks, noting, "I've got a lot of Mexican guys working for me and that's an influence. I always take pleasure in my younger colleagues."

He encourages those new to cooking to come to it with a relaxed attitude. "People shouldn't be nervous to cook. You can roll with what shows up." Bill clearly takes his own advice and rolls with what shows up to make delicious, inspired food.

## Bill's Mint Sorbet

No two batches of this are ever the same. Fresh mint varies in flavor and strength. In late spring and early summer, Mrs. Andrews has a variety with red stems and a kind of herby fragrance that is my favorite. That sorbet is light pink in color. Makes about a quart and a half.

4 cups sugar

8 cups water

2 lemons, zested

8 cups fresh mint leaves, lightly packed

2 cups fresh lemon juice

*Combine the sugar and water in a non-reactive pot and bring to a boil. Add the lemon zest. Boil for about 5 minutes until it looks a little thick and shiny. It almost looks oily to me when it's right. Remove from heat, add the mint leaves and submerge them. Cover and let steep for at least half an hour. Longer is fine. Add the lemon juice and strain the mixture. Chill (if you have time) and churn in your ice cream freezer. It's fine as a sorbet but better as the beginning of a mint julep.*

# · SUMMER ·

# 4

## Berries

Before we built our farmhouse, we planted blueberry bushes in the yard. The house site, recently excavated, displaced much of the topsoil, and the whole area revealed clumpy, rocky, red clay. Layering the planting holes with compost and coffee grounds, we forged ahead. As we worked on the weekends to construct our house, the berries thrived. Lucky for us, blueberries don't really mind poor soil. When friends and family came to help with construction, they nibbled on berries and picked a few quarts to take home. By the time we finished our house, several years later, we were being rewarded with prolific blueberry crops.

I would take them to our bakery along with wild wineberries, blackberries and mulberries collected in the forest around the house. There they turned into pies, scones, muffins, cakes and salads. Berries freeze beautifully, and when my husband picked them by the gallon, we rinsed them, poured them into bags and put them in the freezer to use well into autumn.

When we sold the bakery, we suddenly had the enviable dilemma of too many berries. I canned them, packed our home freezer to bursting and gave quarts to the neighbors. Finally, I called my friend Greg, who owns The Hop Ice Creamery with his wife, Ashley, in Asheville, and he bought the rest of our crop.

Many of the recipes in this chapter were developed during that glorious glut of berries. And my favorite lesson from that time of plenty is you can't ever have too many berries because they can always become ice cream.

## Berry Lemon Tea and Cocktails

My very creative neighbor Vanessa came over for some front porch berry lemon tea on a hot summer evening, and we ended up in the kitchen mixing that tea with everything we could think of. Vanessa is a connoisseur of fine flavors and kept suggesting different combinations. The more we tasted, the more creative we became. Luckily, I was writing down our formulas, because the more creative we got the less I remembered. The tea is delicious on its own, but if you are in the mood, try some of the concoctions we came up with. See more variations on page 52.

### BERRY LEMON TEA

4 cups water, divided
2 berry-flavored teabags (herbal or black)
⅓ cup sugar

I lemon
I cup any kind of berry

*Bring 2 cups of water to a boil. In a pitcher or large jar, combine teabags and boiling water and steep for 5 minutes. Squeeze out and discard teabags. Add in sugar and stir well to combine. Peel zest off the lemon in thin strips, cut in half and squeeze out the juice. Add in remaining cool water, zest and juice from the lemon. Add the berries. Serve over ice. Makes 5 cups*

### BERRY LEMON COCKTAIL

I ounce gin, brandy, whiskey or rum
½ cup Berry Lemon Tea

*Combine and pour over ice.*

## BERRY SANGRIA

½ cup red wine
½ cup Berry Lemon Tea

*Combine and pour over ice.*

## BERRY LIMONCELLO SPRITZER

1 ounce limoncello
½ cup Berry Lemon Tea
½ cup seltzer water

*Combine and pour over ice.*

## MOONSHINE SPRITZER

3 Tablespoons moonshine or corn liquor
1 Tablespoon grenadine
½ cup Berry Lemon Tea
½ cup seltzer water

*Combine and pour over ice.*

## ORANGE BLUSH

1 ounce bourbon
½ ounce Cointreau
½ cup Berry Lemon Tea
2–3 strips of orange zest

*Combine and pour over ice.*

# Strawberry Cornmeal Cakes with Lemon Frosting

### MAKES 10 SMALL CAKES OR 24 CUPCAKES

My business partner Krista found a recipe for vegan berry cornmeal muffins when we were developing recipes for West End Bakery. I wasn't sure how those flavors would combine, but she made them and they were delicious. This version is not at all vegan and is also not a muffin, but it contains that delicious combination of strawberries and cornmeal. The lemon frosting puts them over the top.

## STRAWBERRY CAKES

¾ cup cornmeal
1 ½ cups all-purpose flour
1 ½ teaspoons baking powder
½ teaspoon salt
1 ¼ cups milk, soy milk or buttermilk

1 cup sugar
1 stick (8 Tablespoons) butter, melted
1 egg
1 teaspoon vanilla extract
1 ¼ cups sliced strawberries

*Preheat oven to 350 degrees. Grease 10 (3-inch) mini cake pans or jumbo muffin tins. In a large bowl, sift together the cornmeal, flour, baking powder and salt. In another bowl, whisk together the milk, sugar, melted butter, egg and vanilla. Make a hole in the center of your dry ingredients and pour the wet ingredients in. Fold the wet and dry together until just mixed. Fold the strawberries into the batter. Do not over mix.*

*Scoop batter into greased cake tins and bake for 25–30 minutes, until centers are firm and a toothpick inserted comes out clean. Allow cakes to cool in pans for 15 minutes before removing from the pan. Cool completely before frosting.*

## LEMON CREAM CHEESE FROSTING

1 stick (8 Tablespoons) butter
8 ounces cream cheese
1 ½ cups powdered sugar

1 lemon, finely grated zest, and juice
1 teaspoon vanilla extract

*Using the whip attachment on an electric mixer, whip together the butter and the cream cheese. Add the powdered sugar and mix on low to incorporate. Scrape down sides of the bowl; add lemon and vanilla. Whip frosting for 1–2 minutes until ingredients are incorporated and frosting is fluffy.*

# Oat Griddle Cakes with Maple Berry Syrup

MAKES 12–16 CAKES

My friend Trina told me her kids always liked her pancakes; she has been making the same recipe from *Joy of Cooking* forever. When she made these, they said this recipe was better than her old one. So now she has a new griddle cake recipe. It requires a little pre-planning, but these cakes are perfect with berry syrup or any kind of fruit. Only try it if you are ready to ditch your old pancake recipe.

## THE NIGHT BEFORE

2¼ cups milk or soy milk
½ cup rolled oats

*Combine. Refrigerate oat and milk mixture overnight or for at least 2 hours.*

## FOR THE BATTER

I egg
¼ cup oil
I cup whole wheat flour
I cup all-purpose flour

2 Tablespoons sugar
2 teaspoons baking powder
½ teaspoon salt

*When you are ready to make the batter, combine the egg and the oil with the oatmeal mixture and whisk well. In a separate bowl, combine the flours, sugar, baking powder and salt. Fold the wet ingredients into the dry ingredients.*

*Heat a griddle to medium hot and grease with butter or oil. Spoon batter onto the pan—about ¼ cup per cake. If batter seems too thick, stir in a Tablespoon or so more milk. Cook until bubbles form on top of cake and begin to pop. Flip cakes and cook on the other side. Serve with Maple Berry Syrup (see page 56) or fresh fruit and whipped cream.*

### OAT OPTIONS

If you are pressed for time, try substituting ⅓ cup ground oat flour for rolled oats instead of soaking oats overnight. You can make your own flour in a food processor or blender using ½ cup rolled oats. The texture will be almost as good. Do not use cooked oats, however, as cooked oats give cakes a gummy texture.

## Maple Berry Syrup

4 cups any kind of berry, fresh or frozen
½ cup maple syrup
1 Tablespoon fresh lemon juice

1 Tablespoon water
½ teaspoon vanilla extract

*Combine all the ingredients in a sauce pan. Cook on medium heat, stirring often for the first 5 minutes. Cook uncovered for 30 minutes, stirring occasionally, until syrup has thickened. Serve hot.*

*Leftovers will keep in the fridge for 2 weeks and should be enjoyed on top of more griddle cakes, waffles, pound cake or ice cream.*

## Strawberry Ice Cream or Pretty Please Vanilla with Berries on Top

I'm always surprised when folks tell me their favorite ice cream is vanilla. My husband is one of those folks. He prefers his fruit, chocolate, candy, nuts and so forth on top of his ice cream instead of inside. It's easier to make that way, but I prefer to put in the extra effort required for fruit-filled ice cream. What follows is hers and his versions of a summertime treat. Makes one quart.

## STRAWBERRY ICE CREAM

2½ cups ripe strawberries
1¼ cups heavy cream
½ cup half-and-half
¾ cup sugar
¼ teaspoon salt
1 teaspoon vanilla extract

*Puree the strawberries in a blender or food processor. Combine with all ingredients and mix well. Pour into your ice cream freezer and freeze according to the machine's instructions.*

## PRETTY PLEASE VANILLA WITH BERRIES ON TOP

1½ cups half-and-half
1½ cups heavy cream
⅔ cup sugar
¼ teaspoon salt
1 Tablespoon vanilla extract
Berries or other fruit for the top

*Simply combine all ingredients (except the berries) and mix well. Pour into your ice cream freezer and freeze according to the machine's instructions. Serve with cobbler, pie or cake or simply enjoy by itself.*

### FREEZING BERRIES

Almost nothing needs to happen to berries before they can be preserved for months in the freezer. Some berries I don't even wash before popping them in a plastic bag and stashing them in the freezer to use in smoothies, tarts, popsicles, muffins and cobblers. I even use my frozen berries to make jam. Taking a little extra time to individually quick freeze (IQF) berries means they won't be one big frozen lump when you want to use them. Simply spread them on a pan in a single layer and freeze them for a couple of hours, then use a spatula to remove them from the pan and put in bags for storage. Use them straight out of the freezer, but once they are thawed, it is better to blend or cook them, because the freezing process can give them a mushy or rubbery texture.

# Cucumber Blueberry Mint Salad

### SERVES 4

In the mountains of North Carolina, my blueberry bushes and my cucumber vines bear fruit simultaneously. I contend that the best flavor combinations occur seasonally. When fruits and vegetables ripen at the same time, it is likely they have been consumed jointly for centuries. As our human taste buds evolved, we began to crave these ripe flavors in combination. Inspiration for this salad and many others came from gazing at the garden.

1 ½ cups blueberries
2 ½ cups (2 medium) diced cucumbers
¼ cup fresh mint or basil, chopped
1–2 cloves garlic, minced
2 Tablespoons lime juice
2 Tablespoons sugar
1 teaspoon salt

*Combine berries, cucumbers and herbs in a bowl. In another bowl, whisk together the garlic, lime juice, sugar and salt. Pour over the berry mixture and gently stir to combine. Refrigerate and allow the salad to marinate for about 15 minutes or up to 1 hour before serving. Serve alongside corn on the cob, Falafel Spiced Green Bean Fritters, Herb Focaccia, Tomato Pie, Shrimp and Peach Ceviche, summer squash pie or black bean and corn fritters.*

# Quick and Easy Berry Jam

One summer, we had an Italian exchange student. She was a nice girl but not always helpful. Sometimes I could get her to help out in the kitchen rolling out fresh pasta or scooping cookies, but often she was on WhatsApp texting with her friends. Luckily, most teenagers do well with positive peer pressure, so when my enthusiastic (cute), helpful nephew came to visit, she began to help more. I even got her to pick blueberries from our loaded-down bushes, which quickly got turned into this delicious jam. Makes five to six half-pint jars.

8 cups (2½ pounds) any kind
  of berry
2 cups sugar
¼ teaspoon salt
2 Tablespoons fresh lemon or
  lime juice

2 Tablespoons water
2–3 Tablespoons cornstarch
  (use 3 if berries are very juicy)

*Mix together berries, sugar and salt in a large sauce pot. Mash berries slightly to release juice. Bring to a boil and simmer, uncovered, for about 10 minutes, stirring occasionally. Meanwhile, mix juice, water and cornstarch, making sure there are no lumps in your mixture. Slowly pour cornstarch mixture into jam—stirring constantly—and return to a simmer for about 5 minutes. Jam will thicken.*

*You can blend the jam for a smoother consistency if desired. Jam can be cooled and refrigerated or frozen at this point. It will keep in the fridge for approximately 2 weeks and in the freezer for up to a year. I don't recommend canning this type of jam because the color and texture does not hold up well in that setting.*

### SEEDY BERRIES

If you are using berries with lots of crunchy seeds (wild blackberries, raspberries or wineberries), you may enjoy the texture of your jam more if you combine those berries with strawberries or blueberries, which don't typically have crunchy seeds. You can also use a sieve to strain some of the seeds out of your berries before making jam.

# *Fingerprint Jam Cookies*

We often have three to four varieties of jam open at the same time. This can cause all kinds of problems. We have a smallish fridge, so they get in the way, and God forbid one jar gets shoved in the back of the fridge and molds. It makes me want to cry when all those hours of berry picking and canning end up in the compost. A simple solution to too much jam is to make these cookies. They will keep for a good long time, but I don't know exactly how long because they always get gobbled up.

1 ½ sticks (12 Tablespoons) butter
½ cup sugar
2 egg yolks
½ teaspoon vanilla extract

¼ teaspoon lemon extract
¼ teaspoon salt
2 cups all-purpose flour
½–¾ cup jam or jelly

*Preheat oven to 325 degrees. Cream butter and sugar together using the paddle attachment on a mixer. Beat in egg yolks 1 at a time. *Reserve the egg whites for another use (like meringue cookies?). Add extracts and salt; gradually add the flour. Dough will be quite stiff.*

*Lightly grease cookie sheets and roll dough into balls, about 2 teaspoons of dough, or the size of a small quail egg. Use a finger (or the top of a tiny liquor bottle) and press in the center of each ball. Put about ¼ teaspoon of jam in the center of each cookie. Bake 12–15 minutes. Cookies will still be light in color, with golden-brown bottoms. Cool on racks. Makes 40 to 45 cookies.*

## WHY FINGERPRINT INSTEAD OF THUMBPRINT?

If you use your thumb to make indentions in cookies, you end up with a lopsided indention that jam can leak out from. Using a finger (or mini bottle top) perpendicular to the baking sheet means you have a uniform hole to place your jam. My neighbor Greta tried these using peanut butter and Nutella. PB&J cookies anyone?

# INTERVIEW WITH CHEF APRIL McGREGOR

April McGregor owns and operates Farmer's Daughter in Hillsborough, North Carolina, founded in 2007. She makes pickles and preserves that popularize and promote old southern recipes.

April learned from the best—her mother and grandparents. Growing up on a farm in rural Mississippi, she began cooking as a small child. "Everyone cooked all the time; there was literally no place to eat out," she explains earnestly. Her grandparents had the family over for big meals made from what they grew on their farm, with fresh, purple field peas, okra, greens and cornbread.

Preserving regional cooking techniques is important to April. "Otherwise food gets homogenized and is boring. These regional distinctions make southern food unique. It makes life interesting."

Her tip for novice canners? Start small. Small-batch canning doesn't have to take all weekend. "You can even break the process down over a few days, prep all your vegetables the day before and then it's not overwhelming." April encourages people to use what they have on hand if they are just starting to make their own preserves. "Ferment things a quart at a time. You don't have to invest in special equipment."

April's passion for keeping culinary techniques and traditions alive is equaled by her passion for high-quality, delicious jams, jellies, sauces and pickles. Her community is the lucky beneficiary of both the product and process of these passions.

# 5
## Tomatoes

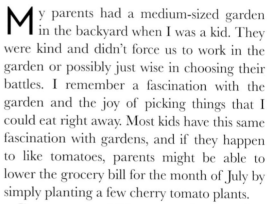

My parents had a medium-sized garden in the backyard when I was a kid. They were kind and didn't force us to work in the garden or possibly just wise in choosing their battles. I remember a fascination with the garden and the joy of picking things that I could eat right away. Most kids have this same fascination with gardens, and if they happen to like tomatoes, parents might be able to lower the grocery bill for the month of July by simply planting a few cherry tomato plants.

I've seen many children entertain themselves for a good long time in the tomato patch. At a cookout in our backyard one night, a toddler found the first ripe tomato of the summer, and it happened to be hanging on the vine right at her mouth level. She proceeded to eat it without picking it, and as the juice ran down her chin, we all watched and chuckled. But afterward, I wondered who wouldn't want to have delicious food presented to them, fresh as can be, mouth level?

I must admit to quite a bit of snacking as I harvest tomatoes, and I encourage kids and adults alike to do the same. If any tomatoes actually make it into the kitchen, there are endless ways to prepare them. They are technically a fruit and therefore can be frozen without blanching or cooking. Having a fairly high acid content makes them perfect for canning; they dry well and bake up into the best savory pies imaginable. The recipes included here will take you from the very beginning of tomato season, enjoying the first ones off the vine, to the end of the season, using up every last green tomato.

## Pesto Tomato Pie

### SERVES 4–6

Don't skip pre-baking the crust here. Even though you are salting and draining the tomatoes, it will still be juicy and messy, so if you pre-bake the crust, you can avoid raw crust syndrome. Juicy and messy are never bad things as long as you don't have a soggy bottom. As a matter of fact, my friend Stephanie thought juicy and messy was so good she made this pie four times in one week.

| | |
|---|---|
| 1 9-inch pie crust | ¼ cup pesto (see page 40), divided |
| 5 cups (1 ½ pounds) sliced tomatoes | 1 cup freshly grated Asiago cheese, divided |
| 1 teaspoon salt | ½ cup diced red onion |

*Preheat oven to 350 degrees. Roll out pie crust and fit into a 9-inch pie pan. Prick the bottom of the crust with a fork or use pie weights to weigh down the crust. Bake for 10 minutes. Meanwhile, slice tomatoes and combine with salt in a strainer set over a bowl. Shake occasionally to encourage draining. Allow tomatoes to release moisture for about 20 minutes, capturing juice for future sauces or salad dressings. Remove crust from the oven and spread about 3 Tablespoons of the pesto in the bottom of the crust. Sprinkle about half of the cheese on top of the pesto. Add red onions on top of cheese. Layer on tomatoes and sprinkle with remaining cheese. Bake for 45 minutes.*

*Remove from the oven and smear the remaining pesto on the top of the tomatoes. Serve with Corn Salad, corn on the cob, cucumber salad, Stuffed Squash Blossoms, Chilled Cucumber Soup, Marinated Summer Squash Salad or Toasted Peanut Green Beans.*

# *Savory Tomato Cobbler*

SERVES 6

Over the years, I have had several friends reveal the secret to their family tomato pie recipe, and it is always mayonnaise. Depending on the type of mayonnaise, I can be a real hater. I am a biscuit lover, though, so I thought I'd even out mayo-hate with biscuit-love to make a cobbler-like tomato pie. The result is incredibly addictive. The mayo actually works to balance the acid of the tomatoes, and the crisp biscuit is the perfect thing to mop up all the resulting juice.

## FILLING

5 cups (1½ pounds) sliced tomatoes
¾ cup diced red onion or sweet yellow onion
¾ cup mayonnaise
1½ cups grated sharp cheese of any kind

½ teaspoon salt
2–3 teaspoons grated or bottled horseradish (optional)

## BISCUIT TOP

1 stick (8 Tablespoons) cold butter
1¾ cups all-purpose flour
2 teaspoons baking powder
½ teaspoon baking soda

½ teaspoon salt
⅔ cup buttermilk or milk mixed with a little lemon juice

*In a 12-inch deep-dish pie pan or casserole dish, layer about half of the sliced tomatoes. In a separate bowl, combine the onion, mayonnaise, cheese, salt and horseradish. Spread half of this mixture over the tomatoes. Layer the rest of the tomatoes on top of cheese mixture and then top with the rest of the cheese.*

*Preheat the oven to 375 degrees while you make the biscuit top. In a food processor (or a bowl), cut butter into flour and process until it has a sand-like consistency. Add baking powder, soda and salt and mix or pulse to combine. Add milk to flour and gently mix or pulse until just combined.*

*Scoop ¼ cup–sized dollops of biscuit dough onto tomato pie until top is covered with little biscuits. Bake for 45–55 minutes, until biscuits are golden brown and any tomato juice you see is bubbling. Serve with corn on the cob, mixed green salad, Marinated Mustard Dill Potato Salad, coleslaw or Ginger Lime Green Beans.*

*Author photo.*

# Polenta Tomato Pie

SERVES 6

I have a friend (identity not revealed) who hides the leftovers in the back of the fridge when she makes this pie so she can eat them the next day. It's so easy to make that I don't bother hiding the leftovers, I just make more. It's a great entrée to serve if you have a gluten-free friend, because it's gluten-free without trying too hard.

## POLENTA

3½ cups water
1 cup cornmeal
2–3 cloves garlic, finely diced
1 teaspoon salt

1 cup grated Asiago or
  Parmesan cheese
2 ounces cream cheese

## PIE

3 cups (1 pound) sliced tomatoes
1 teaspoon salt
1 Tablespoon olive oil
½ teaspoon fresh ground black pepper

½ cup grated Asiago, Parmesan or
  mozzarella cheese
¼ cup fresh basil leaves, chopped
½ teaspoon crushed red pepper (optional)

*Preheat oven to 350 degrees. Combine sliced tomatoes with 1 teaspoon of salt in a strainer set over a bowl. Shake occasionally to encourage draining. Allow tomatoes to release moisture for about 20 minutes, capturing juice for future sauces or salad dressings.*

*Meanwhile, make polenta. Bring water to a boil in a heavy-bottomed sauce pot. Whisk in cornmeal and continue whisking until there are no lumps. Cook covered for about 10 minutes on low heat, stirring occasionally. Add garlic, salt and cheeses and stir until cheese is melted. Pour into a deep-dish 12-inch pie pan or a 9x13 pan.*

*Make the pie by layering tomato slices on top of polenta. Drizzle with oil; sprinkle with black pepper and cheese. Bake for about 25–35 minutes until cheese is bubbly. Sprinkle fresh basil and crushed red pepper (if desired) on top of pie. Serve with mixed green salad, pesto potato salad, Grilled Summer Squash, grilled chicken or Cucumber Feta Chickpea Salad.*

## WINTERTIME POLENTA TOMATO PIE

If you happen to follow the Roasted Cherry Tomato recipe below, and you happen to freeze some, you are in luck, because you can make this pie all year round. Instead of salting fresh tomatoes, substitute two to three cups of roasted cherry tomatoes (thawed) and spread them on top of the polenta. Add some crushed dried herbs in place of the fresh basil if you like.

# Carolina Red Rice

### SERVES 4-5

I spent a month in Ghana, West Africa, cooking with a traditional Ghanaian cook named Susie. She taught me how to make a delicious dish called Jollof Rice. Jollof is on every menu in every restaurant in Ghana. It is also *amazingly* similar to our traditional Carolina Red Rice. Really, the only major difference is that in Ghana they make it with chicken and cured fish instead of sausage and bacon—yet another reminder that much of our southern cooking pays homage to African roots.

12 ounces spicy sausage

2 slices bacon

1½ cups diced red onion

1 cup long-grain white rice

3 cups (1 pound) pureed tomatoes

1 medium green or red bell pepper, diced

4 cloves garlic, finely diced

1 teaspoon salt

1 teaspoon sugar

½ teaspoon fresh ground black pepper

¼ teaspoon ground red pepper or cayenne

*In a large, heavy-bottomed pot, lightly brown the sausage, sliced or crumbled, and remove from the pan. Leave any remaining grease in the pan. Cook the bacon in the same pot; remove the bacon, but leave the grease in the pan. Sauté the onion in the remaining grease until tender. Rinse the rice in warm water to remove extra starch. Add the rice and all the remaining ingredients to the pot, including the bacon and sausage. Stir well and cook covered on medium-low heat about 20 minutes, stirring occasionally until rice is tender—about 10 more minutes.*

*Taste rice, and add an additional ¼–½ cup boiling water if the rice does not seem cooked all the way through. Serve with collard greens, squash casserole, Corn Chow Chow, Grilled Peach Salsa or Toasted Peanut Green Bean Salad.*

### VEGETARIAN VERSION

Omit the sausage and bacon and substitute 1 Tablespoon vegetable oil for the grease. Add 1 can or 1½ cups cooked red kidney beans and 1 Tablespoon smoked paprika.

## Roasted Cherry Tomatoes

Oh the places you can go with these tomatoes! Cherry tomatoes are the prime example of bountiful harvest that comes in all at once and has to be processed pretty quickly. This is a relatively painless and amazingly delicious way to preserve their sweetness and flavor. They can be kept in the freezer all winter long, and as you pull out bag after bag, you will continue to find new ways to relish them.

4 cups cherry tomatoes, washed
   and stemmed

½ teaspoon salt
2 teaspoons light olive oil

*Preheat oven to 400 degrees. Spread tomatoes out on a large sheet pan. Sprinkle with salt and oil and stir to coat evenly. Roast for 25–35 minutes until tomatoes are starting to brown and liquid that has been released from them is reduced to syrup. See page 74 for ideas on using roasted tomatoes.*

## At This Point You Can

- cool the tomatoes and pack in plastic bags in the freezer
- toss them with greens for a salad
- spread them on bread as a sandwich filling
- toss with hot pasta and sprinkle with Parmesan
- serve them on an antipasto platter

- crumble bacon into them and serve atop arugula
- make them into roasted tomato pesto
- pair them with sharp cheeses and crostini
- put them on a pizza
- use them in Polenta Tomato Pie
- take pictures of them

## Roasting Other Varieties of Tomatoes

Of course, you can roast any kind of tomato. I recommend cutting them into one- to two-inch chunks and following this recipe. Roma and plum tomatoes work well sliced in halves or quarters. You can even use midwinter grocery store tomatoes that often taste like cardboard, and they will turn out caramelized and yummy.

## *Tomato Plates*

I remember the first tomato plate I ever had the luck to come across. I was just a little thing. Being the youngest in a family of six, I can't recall which big person allowed me to sit on their lap and share the warm slices of fresh tomato sprinkled simply with salt and pepper. I ate with my hands and licked the juice as it drizzled down my arm. I still love to eat tomato plates with my hands but have found that most folks

want a fork. Slice tomato into rounds half an inch thick and lay in a single layer on a plate. Crumble cheeses if using and sprinkle evenly on top of tomatoes. Sprinkle all remaining ingredients on top of tomatoes, finishing with fresh ground pepper and salt to taste. Each serves two to four people.

SUMMER

### CLASSIC TOMATO AND BASIL

1 large ripe tomato
¼ cup loosely packed basil leaves,
  thinly sliced

1 Tablespoon extra virgin olive oil
Fresh ground pepper and salt to taste

### CUCUMBER, MINT AND FETA

1 large ripe tomato
1 cup finely diced cucumber
1–2 ounces feta cheese, crumbled

4–5 large mint leaves, thinly sliced
Sea salt

### GOAT CHEESE AND FIG AND BOURBON

1 large ripe tomato
2 ounces goat cheese
2–3 large figs, diced
¼ cup loosely packed basil leaves,
  thinly sliced

½ teaspoon bourbon or balsamic vinegar
Fresh ground black pepper and salt

### OLIVES, ORANGE ZEST AND OREGANO

1 large ripe tomato
¼ cup Italian or Greek olives, diced
1 Tablespoon orange zest
1 Tablespoon fresh-squeezed orange juice

1 teaspoon oregano leaves, thinly sliced (½
  teaspoon dried)
⅛ cup shaved Parmesan cheese

### PESTO AND PARMESAN

1 large ripe tomato
2–3 Tablespoons pesto, thinned with a little
  water if necessary

⅛ cup shaved Parmesan cheese
Red pepper flakes, to taste

# Sungold Tomato Pesto

The first time I tried making tomato pesto, I didn't cook the tomatoes. It looked awful. It was runny and separated with a thick glob of stuff at the top of the bowl and watery stuff on the bottom. I must admit it still tasted pretty darn good, so I tried again and cooked my tomatoes to condense some of the juice. It worked like a charm. My sweet momma always says, "If at first you don't succeed, try, try again."

2 cups Sungold cherry tomatoes, or any variety tomato

1 cup Parmesan cheese, fresh is best

2 cloves garlic, crushed and peeled

1 Tablespoon extra virgin olive oil

½ teaspoon salt

*Put tomatoes in a sauce pot on the stove and cook on medium heat for 15–20 minutes. Stir often in the first few minutes of cooking until tomatoes release their juice. Once the juice releases, simmer uncovered until most of the tomato liquid is gone.*

*Puree all ingredients together in a food processor or blend with a mortar and pestle. Makes 1 cup. Serve alongside fritters, toss with pasta, smear on chicken and roasted vegetables or use as a sandwich condiment.*

---

### SUNGOLD TOMATOES

Orange is my favorite color, so it makes sense that my favorite tomato would be bright orange. It's not just the color that makes this variety of cherry tomato the darling of home gardeners. Juicy sweet Sungolds are some of the most prolific tomatoes I've ever grown, and the flavor is closer to candy than vegetable. If you have a tiny patch of ground and any inclination to grow something delicious, I recommend getting a few seeds or a Sungold plant at your local market. You may be making pesto for the whole month of August with one vibrant plant.

---

# Green Tomato Apple and Shallot Salad

### SERVES 4

As the weather gets cool and you are pretty sure the tomatoes on the vine will never get red, apple season is going strong. It is a perfect time to make this salad. The tartness of the tomato pairs perfectly with the sweet apple. It's almost like someone planned it this way.

3 cups (1 pound) diced green tomatoes
2 firm red apples, Pink Lady, Gala or Fuji, diced
1 small shallot, finely diced

2 Tablespoons balsamic vinegar
2 teaspoons olive oil
¾ teaspoon salt

*Put all of the ingredients into a pretty bowl and toss gently. Allow to marinate for 30 minutes before serving. Leftovers are tasty for a couple of days. Serve with black bean soup, grilled Brie sandwiches, mashed sweet potatoes, winter squash gratin, Spinach and Sorghum Meatloaf or Herb Focaccia and goat cheese.*

*Author photo.*

## Tomato Chips

I had a total blowout on my bicycle tire one day, amazingly right in front of a bike shop. It turns out it was meant to be in more ways than one. The nice guy at the shop set me up with a new tire and tube, and while waiting, I got to chatting with another customer. She had a big summer garden too and told me about her dried tomatoes. I had made sundried tomatoes with limited success, but she used her

food dehydrator and sliced the tomatoes pretty thin. The result is a crispy, crunchy cracker-like thing that has amazing flavor. I may never buy crackers again!

12–15 Roma-sized tomatoes
1 ½ teaspoons garlic powder granules
1 ½ teaspoons salt

### OPTIONAL ADDITIONS

2 teaspoons dried oregano, basil or thyme
1 teaspoon smoked paprika powder
1 teaspoon cumin powder

1 teaspoon curry powder
Crushed hot pepper flakes
Fresh ground black pepper

*Slice tomatoes into ¼-inch-thick rounds. Lightly oil the trays of a food dehydrator and arrange tomatoes in a single layer. Mix garlic and salt together and sprinkle evenly over tops of tomatoes. Sprinkle with any optional additions. Dry for 18–36 hours (all dehydrators are a bit different), until tomato rounds are crisp and not soft at all. Makes about 3 cups.*

*Munch on chips by themselves; serve with hummus, pesto dip, Winter Squash Dips or cheese; or crumble on top of pastas, salads and soups.*

# INTERVIEW WITH CHEF JOHN STEHLING

Sometimes picky eaters make the best chefs. This is true in the case of John Stehling, chef and co-owner, with his wife, Julie, of Early Girl Eatery and King Daddy's in Asheville, North Carolina.

John grew up outside Winston-Salem, "putting up a lot of food." His family leased land to grow fields of potatoes and vegetable gardens. Every fall, they would gather with neighbors to dig potatoes, process, freeze, can, pickle and dry their harvests. They would even buy a whole cow and have it butchered for the family to eat. John is picky, he says, because he grew up with home cooking, and the authentic flavors he grew up with can't be easily copied. He strives to share many of those same flavors at his restaurants.

John draws on what he calls "simple, mountain-type cooking" for inspiration, working with what he has on hand. "Regional comfort food and the community that it builds means a lot to me." Reminiscing about the way he grew up, he recalls how people in this part of the country grew and processed most of their own food, used what was available and relied on neighbors out of necessity. Today, John keeps those traditions alive, purchasing from local farmers to make regional favorites: squash casserole, garlic potatoes and pork belly.

His secrets for delicious food? "Use good ingredients, use things you have on hand, keep it simple, use some salt, don't bury food in seasoning." While the advice is simple and down-home, getting from "good ingredients" to the mouthwatering dishes served in his restaurants may not be quite so easy. Local ingredients and real community relationships are a good place to start.

## John's Ketchup

10 pounds tomatoes, cored and chopped
3 onions, chopped
2 cups diced red bell peppers
1 teaspoon cinnamon
1 teaspoon paprika
2 teaspoons celery seed

½ teaspoon allspice
½ teaspoon cayenne pepper
1 cup apple cider vinegar
½ cup brown sugar
½ teaspoon salt
½ teaspoon pepper

*Cook tomatoes on medium heat in pot until well stewed (40 minutes). Run tomatoes through a food mill and discard seeds and skins. Puree onions and peppers with 2 cups tomato juice mixture until smooth. Put liquids into pot with cinnamon, paprika, celery seed, allspice and cayenne. Simmer for another hour. Add apple cider vinegar, brown sugar, salt and pepper. Place in canning jars.*

# 6

# Peaches

I was born far from the South, and my family did not settle back here until I was close to four years old. So I clearly recall the first time I had a fresh peach. I had experienced a few commercially canned peaches and liked them well enough, but the round fuzzy fruit was a different animal altogether. Unlike some folks, I was not put off by the downy surface. The peach was so ripe that the skin seemed to slide right away as my little mouth bit down. Immediately, juice began to drip down my arm, but I was too consumed by the sweet nectar-like flavor to notice.

That was the beginning of a lifelong love affair. When the first baskets of peaches start to appear at the farmers' market, I usually snap one up and commence to making everything peachy. Diced peaches mix with yogurt and granola for breakfast, slices top my salads at lunchtime and grilled peaches appear on platters at dinnertime.

Peach season is fleeting, so my kitchen often buzzes with fruit flies in July as I attempt to process, pickle and freeze as many as possible. Only once did I make the mistake of buying a basket of peaches in September. Not wanting the magic to be over, I hoped they would taste like July. The difference was striking. Those colorful but juiceless fruits made sad salsas, shortcakes and salads. I dutifully peeled and froze them, as they at least added body to a smoothie, if not flavor.

That experience led me to reflect that it is possible to enjoy a perfect peach out of season—but only if it has been procured and processed during the season's height. Frozen fruits can make delicious cobblers, sorbets and cakes. Pickled peaches are luscious with roasted meats and cheeses or tossed into salads. Versatile peach preserves can go smoky, savory or sweet. Still, my favorite way to eat a peach is straight out of the basket with juice dripping down my arm.

## Tomato Peach Salad

SERVES 4-6

We have a shared driveway that leads up the road to our farm. Unfortunately, the peach tree is on the neighbors' side of the driveway. On the upside, we have the most generous neighbors in the world, and they are happy to share some of their good fortune. I make this salad if I have just one or two perfect peaches that want to get used right away.

2 Tablespoons water
1 teaspoon lime juice
2 medium-sized peaches, peeled and sliced to bite size

8 cups tender lettuce or Mesclun mix
1 cup cherry tomatoes, halved or quartered
⅓ cup Homegrown Herb Vinaigrette (see page 43)

*Mix water and lime juice and pour it over the peaches. Put the lettuce in a salad bowl and top with the tomatoes. Just before serving, put the peaches and juice on the salad and toss with Homegrown Herb Vinaigrette or your favorite balsamic vinaigrette. Serve with Squash Casserole, Pimento Cheese, Sweet Bell Pepper Flatbread or Pesto Tomato Pie.*

## Peach and Elderflower Sorbet

MAKES 1 PINT

The city of Angers southwest of Paris is a great place to ride a bicycle. I happened to be riding around that city on a sunny spring day and, since my French is a tad rusty, got terribly lost. I ended up at a historic distillery that makes more than twenty varieties of liqueur. Needing a break from the bike, I tasted quite a few and fell in love with their elderflower liqueur. Flavors are hard to describe, but this reminded me of

sucking on honeysuckle nectar. I bought a bottle of the elixir and strapped it to my bike, magically finding my way home with no trouble. Since then I have combined it deliciously with citrus and berries, but the magic of that flavor is most apparent when combined with peaches in this sorbet.

½ pound (2 medium) peaches
¼ cup sugar
2 Tablespoons elderflower liqueur
  (such as St. Germaine)

1 teaspoon lemon juice
Pinch salt

*Peel and quarter peaches. Combine with other ingredients in a container with a lid and freeze for 1 hour. Puree everything, return to the container and freeze for 1–2 hours or more before serving, depending on the temperature of your freezer. Eat immediately after serving. Because of the alcohol, the sorbet will melt quickly. Serve in tiny scoops as an elegant end to a shrimp boil or any other summertime soirée.*

## Shrimp and Peach Ceviche

### SERVES 6–8 AS AN APPETIZER

The first time I had ceviche, my mind was blown. I was visiting friends in Belize, and we spent the day on a sailboat in crystal-clear Caribbean coral reefs. When our guide dove off the side and was underwater for several minutes, we began to get anxious. Our relief was palpable when he resurfaced triumphantly, holding a huge conch shell above his head. My friends diced the conch and soaked it in lime juice with a little onion and cilantro. Eating it straight out of the bowl with fresh tortillas, I could not believe what an effect a little lime juice had on that glorious shellfish. Conch is a little harder to find around here, but shrimp works beautifully, and when combined with peaches, I feel like I'm on vacation.

| | |
|---|---|
| 1 pound shrimp | 1 red bell pepper, finely diced |
| 4 Tablespoons (2 large limes) fresh lime juice | 1 medium jalapeño pepper, finely diced |
| 1 ½ pounds (4–5 medium) firm peaches | ½ cup minced red onion |
| 1 cup cilantro leaves, chopped | 1 teaspoon salt |

*Peel and devein shrimp. Put into a strainer or colander in the sink. Boil about 4 cups of water and pour over the shrimp. This will turn them a little pink. Dice shrimp and combine in a bowl with lime juice. Marinate in the fridge for about 1 hour. Meanwhile, peel and dice peaches and combine with remaining ingredients. Mix in the shrimp and taste. If your peaches are firm they may not be as sweet, so feel free to add a pinch or two of sugar to have the right balance of sweet and tart.*

*Serve with tortilla chips, Grits Soufflé, Hoecakes, Herb Focaccia, grilled pepper corn and black bean salad, Squash Casserole or Polenta Tomato Pie.*

## Grilled Peaches
## Sweet and Savory

*Author photo.*

When I'm done grilling the burgers, veggies, corn and so on, I throw some peaches on for dessert. If I'm using charcoal, this is a great way to use the last of the heat, as it requires little effort and the resulting smoky peaches are incredible with a little vanilla ice cream or all by themselves. Turn any leftover peaches into salsa, slice onto salads or stash in the freezer for a smoky wintertime taste of summer.

GRILLED PEACH SALSA

## HOW TO GRILL A PEACH

Cut the peaches in half and take out the pit. Put them on the grill with the cut side down. Sear for about five minutes, and then turn the peaches over skin-side down and grill for ten to twenty-five more minutes depending on how hot your grill is. The peaches will be smoky and soft when they are done. Juice will form in the place where the pit used to be. Don't spill the juice when you take the peaches off the grill—it is delicious. After peaches have cooled, it is very easy to slip off the fuzzy peel.

2 cups (1 pound whole) grilled peaches
1 large tomato, chunked (about 1 ½ cups)
1 Tablespoon lime juice
2 cloves garlic, finely diced

½ teaspoon salt
½–1 teaspoon chipotle puree or dried
 powder
½ cup cilantro or basil leaves

*Put everything but the cilantro leaves in a food processor and pulse until it is a chunky consistency. Add cilantro and pulse several times to combine. Alternatively, dice tomatoes and peaches and combine with remaining ingredients.*

## Pickled Jalapeño Ginger Peaches

One time my husband mistook these peaches for bourbon peach preserves and put them on vanilla ice cream. It was surprisingly good. I think they go well with just about anything. I even tried one in a Bloody Mary and could not complain at all.

½ pound (2 medium) peaches
¾ cup cider vinegar
3 Tablespoons sugar
1 Tablespoon sliced ginger root

1 cinnamon stick or star anise pod
½ medium jalapeño pepper, seeded
 (optional)

*Peel and slice peaches and put into a very clean pint-sized mason jar. Combine all remaining ingredients in a saucepan and bring to a boil. Pour hot brine over peaches, making sure they are covered. Add a bit more vinegar if needed to cover peaches. Put the lid on the jar and allow to sit on the counter for at least 24 hours before tasting. Will keep on the counter for 1 week, unopened. Once opened, refrigerate; peaches should keep indefinitely.*

*Serve alongside roasted pork or chicken, in a salad with goat cheese and toasted nuts, tossed with cooked rice and toasted cumin seed, with prosciutto and basil, topping aged cheese and crackers or in place of chutney and salsa.*

## Ginger Peach Cake with Whipped Cream

People with summer birthdays have all the fun! This is a great celebration cake. I've also been known to eat it for breakfast, because I do have a summer birthday and I deserve it. Makes one 9x13 cake or two 8-inch cakes.

## CAKE

2½ cups all-purpose or whole wheat pastry
   flour
1½ teaspoons baking powder
½ teaspoon baking soda
½ teaspoon salt
½ cup (8 Tablespoons) butter
1¼ cups sugar

½ cup vegetable oil
4 eggs
¾ cup milk or soy milk
1 teaspoon vanilla extract
2½ cups (1 pound whole) peeled and diced
   peaches
½ cup crystalized ginger, finely diced

*Preheat oven to 350 degrees Sift together the flour, baking powder, soda and salt. In another bowl, or a stand mixer, cream together the butter and sugar. Add in the oil, and mix in the eggs one at a time. Mix in the milk and vanilla. Fold the flour mixture into the wet ingredients, and then fold in the peaches and ginger. Do not over mix.*

*Pour batter into greased pans and bake 30–40 minutes depending on the size of your pan. A toothpick inserted into the center should come out clean. Cool cake(s) completely, remove from pans and frost with whipped cream.*

## WHIPPED CREAM FROSTING

1 pint heavy whipping cream
½ cup powdered sugar

*Combine cream and sugar. Whip with electric beaters or a whisk until cream forms stiff peaks, but do not over whip or you will have sweet butter.*

## Bourbon Basil Peach Preserves

There is something about peaches that seems wicked—seductively juicy, sweet and soft. I like to mix peaches with bourbon, because bourbon is wicked, and together they are wickedly good.

¾ pound (3 medium) peaches
½ cup bourbon, any brand you like
½ cup sugar

1 Tablespoon lemon juice
1 teaspoon vanilla extract
¼ teaspoon salt
3–4 basil leaves, gently crushed in your fist

*Peel and slice peaches and put into 1 quart-sized or 2 pint-sized mason jars. Add all remaining ingredients to the jar, put lid on securely and shake gently for several minutes to dissolve sugar. Add 1–2 more Tablespoons bourbon to the jar if necessary to cover peaches in liquid and shake again. Refrigerate for at least 24 hours. Remove basil leaves, and enjoy for up to 2 months, keeping refrigerated. Serve peaches over ice cream, waffles, pancakes, pound cake, doughnuts and cheesecake or alongside any cheese with crackers or crostini.*

## CANNING BOURBON BASIL PEACHES

For a shelf-stable version, combine all ingredients in a sauce pan and bring to a boil. Remove basil leaves and divide equally between two sanitized pint mason jars. Tightly screw lids on jars.

Bring a large pot of water to a boil and submerge jars in water with at least one inch of water covering jars. Simmer for fifteen minutes. Remove from water and cool completely, testing lids to make sure they are sealed.

NOTE: By heating the bourbon, the alcohol content of the finished product is greatly reduced.

# 7

## Corn

Is it grain or vegetable? Happily, the answer is both.

I spent a summer of my life getting intimate with corn. Working at Gwynn Valley summer camp as the miller proved to be quite an education. I ran a water-powered gristmill from the 1890s, teaching kids the history of corn in Appalachia. Using dent corn (a starchy variety perfect for grinding) grown right there at camp, kids learned to shuck, shell and sift ground corn into cornmeal, grits, corn flour and chaff. Then we would troop outside and make johnnycake, also called hoecake, on the fire. In order to use all the ground corn, I had to get creative and make zucchini bread, carrot cake, blueberry cobbler and corn tortillas. The kids loved learning to mix up batter, cook on the fire and consume our delicious experiments.

In that case, corn was a grain, because the kernels were dried before grinding, but if you eat corn fresh, it is considered a vegetable. Usually, we eat sweet corn fresh and use the much starchier dent corn for grinding. Gwynn Valley grew copious amounts of both varieties, so the kids and I got to play with corn puddings, infused butters, salads and even fish cakes.

I will never regret my love affair with corn, and luckily, my husband isn't the jealous type. Not unlike the kids at summer camp, he's always happy to taste the concoctions that corn and I come up with.

# Carolina Shrimp Boil

SERVES 6-8

For my birthday one year, friends threw me a shrimp boil. Nothing says love like piles of fish, corn and potatoes. Luckily, my birthday is in June, because this decadent dish must be eaten outside. The newspaper rolls out, the food is piled on top and everyone rolls up their sleeves to consume copious amounts of corn on the cob, hot shrimp and frothy cold beverages.

## SHRIMP AND SPICE RUB

2 pounds medium shrimp, unpeeled
1 teaspoon salt

1 teaspoon smoked paprika
1 teaspoon ground black pepper

## SHRIMP BOILING BROTH

5 quarts water
2 Tablespoons salt
6 cloves garlic, crushed and peeled
2 Tablespoons smoked paprika
1 Tablespoon celery seed
1 Tablespoon hot pepper flakes

1 Tablespoon mustard seeds
1 Tablespoon coriander seeds
1 teaspoon ground black pepper
½ teaspoon ground nutmeg
½ teaspoon ginger powder

NOTE: *You can substitute a boil-in-bag seasoning pack (such as Zatarain's) for all the spices, not including salt.*

## THE REST OF IT

6 ears corn, shucked and cut in half
2 pounds red potatoes, washed and quartered
1 pound smoked sausage, cut in 2-inch pieces
1 lemon, juiced
4 Tablespoons butter

Combine shrimp with salt, paprika and pepper 1–2 hours before cooking. Refrigerate until ready to cook. Combine water and spices in a large pot and bring to a boil. Add corn, potatoes and sausage to water, bring to a boil and cook for 5–8 minutes. Taste a potato; cook a few more minutes if necessary, until the potatoes are done.

Add the shrimp to the pot and stir until all the shrimp turn pink, about 30 seconds, then drain the cooking water from the pot—reserving it for delicious soup stock or rice cooking liquid.

Put everything back in the pot and combine with lemon juice, butter and salt to taste. Transfer to a large bowl or spread on clean newspaper for serving. Serve with lots of condiments for dipping on the side.

## SHRIMP BOIL CONDIMENT SUGGESTIONS

- Fresh Herb Remoulade (see page 151)
- Parsley Caper Butter (see page 99)
- Spicy Pickled Onions (see page 207)
- Roasted Red Pepper Sauce (see page 123)
- Garlic Mustard Butter (see page 98)
- pesto (see page 40)
- lemon wedges
- salt

# CORN ON THE COB AND SLATHERINGS

Arguably, the best way to eat corn is straight off the cob with something delicious slathered on it. I like to make up several of these corn toppings and serve a big bowl of steaming hot corn cobs, snapped in half, so folks can eat several pieces with different flavors on each one. See pages 98–99 for slatherings.

## COOKING CORN ON THE COB

GRILLING: Grill in the husks on medium-high heat for about fifteen minutes, turning every three to five. Allow to cool slightly and carefully remove the husks and silks.

BOILING: Shuck the corn and remove the silks. Bring a pot of water to a boil and add the corn. Bring back to a boil and remove from heat. Corn can sit in hot water for up to fifteen minutes before serving, or it can be served right away.

MICROWAVE: Do not shuck the corn—simply put it whole into the microwave. For one ear, two to three minutes on high should do it. Increase the time depending on how many ears you are doing at once. Be careful—it will be quite hot when it is done. Let it cool for about ten minutes before shucking it. You can also wear gloves to shuck it. The husks and silks come off quite easily.

## Slatherings, Infused Butters and Such

For the following recipes containing butter, soften butter by heating for a few seconds in the microwave or leave out at room temperature for an hour (as long as your room is 70 degrees or more). When butter is the consistency of pudding, it is perfect for stirring with other ingredients.

### AVOCADO "BUTTER"

I small avocado, pureed
I garlic clove, crushed
I teaspoon lemon or lime juice
½ teaspoon salt

### CHIPOTLE LIME BUTTER

4 Tablespoons softened salted butter
I ½ teaspoons lime juice
½ teaspoon chipotle puree
2 pinches salt

### BLUE CHEESE AND BACON INFUSED MAYO

2 Tablespoons mayonnaise
¼ cup crumbled blue cheese
2 slices bacon, cooked and crumbled
½ teaspoon lemon juice

### FRESH HERB MAYO

¼ cup mayonnaise
I clove garlic, finely diced
2 Tablespoons minced parsley
I Tablespoon minced rosemary or sage
I teaspoon lemon juice
⅛ teaspoon salt

### BASIL LIME MAYO

¼ cup mayonnaise
¼ cup basil leaves, minced
 (2 Tablespoons dried)
2 teaspoons fresh lime juice
⅛ teaspoon salt

### GARLIC MUSTARD BUTTER

4 Tablespoons softened salted butter
2 cloves garlic, finely diced
I teaspoon stone ground or Dijon mustard
I pinch salt

## MUSTARD ANCHOVY BUTTER

4 Tablespoons softened salted butter
1 teaspoon anchovy paste
   (or 2 filets, mashed)
1 teaspoon Dijon mustard

## NASTURTIUM BUTTER

4 Tablespoons softened salted butter
4-5 nasturtium flowers, diced

## ORANGE MUSTARD BUTTER

4 Tablespoons softened salted butter
1 Tablespoon orange zest
1 teaspoon orange juice
1 teaspoon stone ground or
   Dijon mustard

## ORANGE ROSEMARY BUTTER

4 Tablespoons softened salted butter
1 Tablespoon orange zest
1 teaspoon orange juice
1 teaspoon chopped fresh rosemary
2 pinches salt

## PARSLEY CAPER BUTTER

4 Tablespoons softened salted butter
1 Tablespoon minced capers
1 Tablespoon minced parsley

## PESTO BUTTER

4 Tablespoons softened salted butter
2 Tablespoons prepared pesto

## ROASTED RED PEPPER BUTTER

4 Tablespoons softened salted butter
¼ cup roasted red peppers, minced

## ROASTED TOMATO BUTTER

4 Tablespoons softened salted butter
¼ cup Roasted Cherry Tomatoes
   (see page 73), minced

## SMOKED SEA SALT AND GARLIC BUTTER

4 Tablespoons softened unsalted butter
2 cloves garlic, finely diced
½ teaspoon smoked sea salt

# Ricotta Grits Soufflé

SERVES 6

I threw a brunch for my nephew Patrick the day after he got married. It was October in the mountains, meaning pretty chilly. Our house is rather small, and we couldn't count on spilling out to the front porch. My husband suggested we draw the line at thirty invites. Well, apparently word got out at the wedding that there was to be a brunch at my house in the morning. Luckily, I had prepared huge vats of this soufflé, along with corn and bacon salsa, black-eyed peas, fresh spinach artichoke dip and Potato Mushroom Custard Pie. When pretty much everyone showed up at my house, we had a grand time and no one went hungry, but there was not a scrap of soufflé left.

4 cups water

1 cup yellow corn grits

1¼ teaspoons salt

1 cup grated sharp Cheddar

1 cup ricotta or goat cheese

2 cloves garlic, finely diced

5 eggs, yolks separated

*In a heavy-bottomed sauce pan, bring the water to a boil. Pour in grits while stirring, gradually, so that no lumps form. Turn heat to medium and cook the grits 20 minutes, stirring every few minutes. Remove from heat and stir in salt, cheeses and garlic. Set aside to cool 30 minutes—see note about pre-making grits.*

*Preheat oven to 350 degrees. While grits are cooling, thoroughly butter a 3-quart deep-dish soufflé dish or an 7x11 glass dish depending on your style. Using an electric mixer or a very strong arm, whisk egg whites until they form stiff peaks. Stir egg yolks into grits. Stir about half of the whites into the grits, and then gently fold the remaining whites into the grits. Pour into prepared pan. Bake about 30 minutes, until puffed and golden.*

*Serve with salsas, sauces, beans, eggs, sautéed greens, sausage, bacon or roasted vegetables.*

### MAKE THE GRITS THE NIGHT BEFORE

If you plan to serve this soufflé in the morning and want to speed up the process, you can make the grits the night before and leave them out to cool. You can even make the grits a couple of days beforehand and keep them in the fridge until ready to make soufflé. You can even use leftover grits if you've got enough!

# Corn Chow Chow

I am often asked, "What is chow chow?" The answer is simple and complex. Chow chow is a pickled relish, but it can be made with a huge variety of vegetables, from beets to cucumbers, asparagus and carrots to green tomatoes, peaches or peas. It is served as a condiment and is particularly good served with beans or field peas but is also great with casseroles or tacos. Chow chow's origins are far-flung, possibly India or China, but it has settled in quite nicely in the South.

½ cup pickled vegetables (green beans, squash or cucumber)
1½ cups cooked corn kernels (1 large cob)
½ cup thinly sliced carrot
½ cup diced bell pepper, any color
½ cup diced onion

2 cloves garlic, thinly sliced
¼ cup cider vinegar
1 Tablespoon sugar
1 teaspoon salt
1 teaspoon finely grated fresh ginger
½ teaspoon ground coriander

*Combine everything in a bowl and refrigerate for 3–4 hours. Serve alongside beans, roasted meat and grilled sandwiches, with tortilla chips and on top of soups or a nice juicy hot dog. Chow chow will keep refrigerated for several weeks.*

## Hoecakes

Hoecakes were originally cooked over an open fire on the metal head of a hoe. They may have been made simply with cornmeal and water, because sometimes that was the only food available. Other ingredients were added in if they were on hand. I have made them with cornmeal and water only, but this version is quite a bit more flavorful, and with each additional ingredient I add I am  reminded of human tenacity and my own good fortune. Hoecakes are simple and quick to make, so if you realize your bread is moldy or you don't have crackers in the house, whip up a batch. As you heat your skillet indoors on your stove, be reminded of the indomitable human spirit and count your blessings.

1 egg
½ cup milk, buttermilk, soy milk or water
1 Tablespoon vegetable or olive oil
1 cup cornmeal

1 teaspoon baking powder
½ teaspoon salt
1 teaspoon bacon grease or vegetable oil, for frying

### OPTIONAL ADDITIONS

½ teaspoon fresh ground black pepper
1 Tablespoon chopped fresh sage
1 ½ teaspoons dried herbs

½ cup grated cheese
¼ teaspoon ground chilies
1–2 Tablespoons sugar or honey

*Whisk together egg, milk and oil; add remaining ingredients—except for grease—and mix well. Heat a skillet on medium-high heat and add grease or oil to the pan.*

*Fry cakes for about 2 minutes on each side. Cakes can be any size depending on how you are serving them. If you want a bit of a flipping challenge, fry all the batter at once and then cut into wedges to serve. Hoecakes are best eaten hot off the griddle. They do dry out after a few hours, so eat them while they are fresh or toast day-old cakes before serving.*

*Serve with soups, salads, spreads, salsas and chili or spread some sorghum on them for an authentic Appalachian treat.*

# Corn Salad

SERVES 6–8

Every once in a while, I get the enviable job of passing out free produce at one of the local elementary schools. I stand in front of school as kids are being picked up or loading on buses, giving away grocery bags for them to fill with corn, green beans, tomatoes, peppers and potatoes. I love watching kids get excited about vegetables. I like to hand out this recipe along with the veggies, 'cause it is hard to find a kid who isn't excited about corn.

5–6 ears of corn, cooked (6–8 cups)
3 cups raw veggies, cut into bite-sized
   pieces (cherry tomatoes, bell peppers,
   cucumbers and so forth)
2 cloves garlic, finely diced

2 Tablespoons extra virgin olive oil
1 teaspoon salt
¼ cup crumbled feta or ½ cup finely diced
   Monterey Jack cheese (optional)

*Cut cooked corn off of the cob by standing corn vertically and slicing off kernels. To "milk" the corn, hold knife perpendicular to cob after all kernels have been taken off and scrape downward to release remaining edible bits.*

*In a bowl, combine corn with other vegetables. Add remaining ingredients and gently toss to combine. Serve alongside Falafel Spiced Green Bean Fritters, Chilled Cucumber Soup, Pesto Tomato Pie or pimento cheese toast.*

# INTERVIEW WITH CHEF ANDREA REUSING

"Taste is pretty subjective right? So a really crispy fish skeleton could be the most delicious thing in the world if we adjust our own perceptions about what flavor is." Andrea Reusing, chef and owner of Lantern restaurant in Chapel Hill and The Durham in Durham, North Carolina, describes her source of inspiration as an extension of her belief system. "Just because a dish is exotic or uses 'luxury' ingredients doesn't mean I want to have it on the menu." For her, taste is about using products that are locally available and making them delicious. She points out that sometimes there are ingredients that need to be used that we don't think of as alluring, and the challenge is how to change people's perception of taste so that we use what we have on hand.

"Cooking is most exciting for me when I'm solving a problem," the chef explains in her typical straightforward fashion. Andrea believes that whether you're dealing with scarcity or bounty, the same problem exists: cooking and preserving food in a way that makes sense. "How to deal with all these strawberries all at once or all this corn all at once gets overlooked in the hyped-up enthusiasm about food. So much of cooking, at its best, is about fixing a problem."

Trial and error become tools that most chefs, including Andrea, employ to stimulate the creative process. "Maybe sometimes at the tail end of the season you find the perfect way to preserve something, and you end up waiting a whole year to do it again." Different parts of the harvest are also ideal for different things. "At the restaurant, we figured out which dishes to make at the beginning of tomato season, what we do in the middle and what dishes to make at the end of tomato season as we are approaching needing to do more preservation."

Andrea explores this process and how it works for her personally in her book *Cooking in the Moment: A Year of Seasonal Recipes*. Her approach to cooking with fresh seasonal produce while simultaneously pursuing an influential career and raising a family is inspiring and alluringly tasty.

# Andrea's Crispy Corn Fritters

## MAKES 30 SMALL FRITTERS

*From* Cooking in the Moment: A Year of Seasonal Recipes *by Andrea Reusing*

These are good as a savory side or drizzled with honey or sorghum for breakfast.

5 to 6 ears of corn, shucked

2 large eggs

Kosher salt

¾ cup all-purpose flour

½ teaspoon baking powder

⅛ teaspoon cayenne

Vegetable oil, for frying

*On a large plate, using the coarse holes of a box grater, grate 5 ears of corn with swift downward strokes (to avoid the fiber from the cob). Be sure to catch all the milk. Measure the corn mixture and, if necessary, continue with the last ear to make exactly 1 cup corn. Transfer it to a medium bowl.*

*Separate the eggs over a small bowl, allowing the whites to fall into the bowl and adding the yolks to the corn. With a fork, combine the yolks, corn and ½ teaspoon salt. Sift the flour, baking powder and cayenne directly onto the corn mixture and mix to combine.*

*Pour 2 inches of oil into a large, deep skillet, making sure that the oil does not fill the pan more than halfway, and heat over low heat. Meanwhile, beat the egg whites to soft peaks and gently fold them into the corn mixture. Raise the heat under the skillet to medium, and heat until the oil reaches 350°F on a deep-fat thermometer.*

*Working with two small Tablespoons, carefully lay about 10 dollops of batter into the hot oil— fewer if they begin to crowd the pan. Fry for 2 to 3 minutes, until golden brown, flipping them about halfway through cooking. Transfer the fritters with a slotted spoon directly onto a clean brown paper bag to drain. Repeat with the remaining batter. Season with salt to taste and serve immediately.*

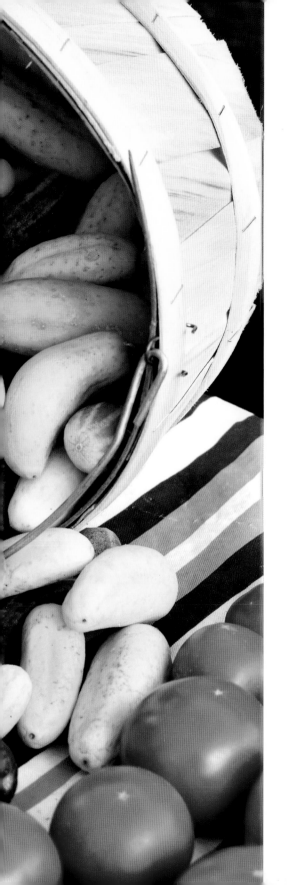

# 8

## Cucumbers

Years ago I started a little garden behind our bakery/café. I grew mostly herbs so that we could run out and grab fresh parsley or rosemary for our soups and salads, but every summer, I grew a few cucumbers up the little wooden fence surrounding the garden.

When the kitchen hubbub died down for the day, I escaped to the garden to search for cucumbers. They like to play hide-and-go-seek, but they are always the ones hiding. Following the vines along the fence line and lifting up the big leaves, the game was a nice distraction. I would often gather basketfuls of those prolific fruits, dreaming up all the ways I would use them as I hauled them back to the kitchen.

Cucumbers present an interesting culinary challenge in that they do not like to be heated. At the bakery, I would often roast vegetables when they passed their prime, crisping and caramelizing them into deliciousness. That was not an option with the slightly aged cucumber. I had to get creative. Luckily, cucumbers play nicely with lots of other flavors, so they became a backdrop for many a salad dressing, while fresher counterparts were the star ingredient in salads themselves. A particularly large haul of cucumbers meant that I made refrigerator pickles that could last for weeks and still be crunchy. This chapter includes many of the recipes I've developed over the years to enjoy the summer glut of cucumbers without wasting a single one.

## Cucumber Cocktails and Spritzers

A couple of my friends helped me test out every single one of these recipes, bless their hearts. It was a tough job, but they didn't seem to mind one bit. Of course you can substitute your favorite seltzer water, club soda or just plain water in these concoctions if you want a refreshing nonalcoholic beverage. Some of the recipes are infusions and need to sit for a day to soak up that cucumber flavor. You can always let them sit for longer than a day; they will only get better. Each recipe makes about four drinks.

## LEMON CUCUMBER INFUSED GIN

1 medium (12 ounces) cucumber, zebra
  peeled and sliced into rounds
1¼ cups gin

½ lemon, sliced into rounds
¼ cup sugar

*Put ingredients in a jar, making sure that the fruit is immersed; add a bit more gin if you need to. Stir to dissolve the sugar. Refrigerate for 12–24 hours or up to a week.*

## CITRUS CUCUMBER GIN FIZZ

1 cup Lemon Cucumber Infused Gin (see recipe)
2 cups sparkling lemonade, limeade, Orangina or seltzer
Ice

*Mix gin with soda. Pour over ice into glasses and garnish with lemons and cucumbers from the infusion.*

## CUCUMBER ORANGE GINGER INFUSED VODKA

1¼ cups vodka
1 medium cucumber, zebra peeled and
   sliced into rounds

1 orange, sliced
1 inch ginger root, sliced
¼ cup sugar

*Put ingredients in a jar, making sure that the fruit is immersed; add a bit more vodka if you need to. Stir to dissolve the sugar. Refrigerate for 12–24 hours or up to a week.*

## CUCUMBER LIME MINT JULEP OR MINT SPRITZER

¾ cup sugar
2 cups water, divided
2 medium (1½ pounds) cucumbers
1 cup fresh mint leaves

1 lime, juiced
1 cup bourbon or seltzer
Crushed ice
Mint leaves for garnish

*Make simple syrup in a sauce pot by combining the sugar and 1½ cups water; bring to a simmer, stir to dissolve and allow to cool. Puree the cucumber in a blender or food processor. Combine the cucumber, mint and lime juice and use a potato masher or muddler to crush the mint leaves. Add ½ cup water to the mint mixture, stir and pour through a strainer—discard the solids. Combine the simple syrup with the mint mixture.*

*Make juleps with 2 parts mint mixture and 1 part bourbon or seltzer poured over ice and garnished with mint leaves.*

SUMMARY

# SUMMER

## CUCUMBER SCREWDRIVER

1 cup Cucumber Orange Ginger Infused
 Vodka (see recipe)
2 cups orange juice

1 cup seltzer
Ice

*Mix vodka, juice and seltzer and pour into glasses over ice. Garnish with fruit from the vodka.*

## FROZEN CUCUMBER MARGARITA OR LIMEADE SLUSHY

2 medium (1½ pounds) cucumbers, peeled,
 seeded and chunked
4 large limes
1 cup tequila

½ cup triple sec
¼ cup agave syrup or sugar
2 cups crushed ice
Kosher salt for glasses

*Place cucumber chunks on a plate and freeze for about an hour or up to 24 hours. Remove zest and juice from 3 limes and reserve the other lime for serving. In a blender, puree cucumbers, lime zest, lime juice, tequila, triple sec, sugar and ice.*

*For limeade, substitute lime seltzer for tequila and triple sec; add additional agave syrup to taste.*

*Slice the last lime into wedges and rub rims of glasses, dip in salt, pour frozen margarita into salt-rimmed glasses and garnish with lime.*

## BASIL CUCUMBER MOJITO OR SPRITZER

2 medium (1½ pounds) cucumbers
1 cup fresh basil leaves
1 lime, juiced
½ cup sugar

1 cup water
1 cup white rum or seltzer water
Basil for garnish

*Puree the cucumber in a blender or food processor. Combine cucumber, basil, lime and sugar and use a potato masher or muddler to crush the basil leaves. Add the water, stir, pour through a strainer and discard the solids. Add rum or seltzer and pour over ice, garnishing with fresh basil leaves.*

## Cucumber Dressings and Sauces

I might be tooting my own horn, but to my good friends I am known as the "Dressing Goddess." We're not talking about polka dots or pinstripes—we're talking salad dressing. I always have big jugs of homemade concoctions in my fridge for the impromptu salad. I discovered years ago that cucumbers puree and emulsify dressings beautifully, and they pretty much go with anything in this form, even polka dots.

### CUCUMBER BUTTERMILK RANCH

1 medium cucumber, peeled and cut in chunks (about 1 ½ cups)

½ cup buttermilk

½ cup sour cream

¼ cup mayonnaise

3 cloves garlic, crushed and peeled

2 Tablespoons fresh basil (1 Tablespoon dried)

1 Tablespoon fresh oregano (½ Tablespoon dried)

½ teaspoon salt

½ teaspoon sugar

*Put everything in the blender and blend well. Serving suggestions: cucumber salads, as a sauce for pizza, dip for veggies, with burgers and fries, lettuce salads, coleslaw, in grilled potato packs.*

## CUCUMBER TOMATO BASIL

1 medium cucumber, peeled and cut in
  chunks (about 1 ½ cups)
1 cup chopped tomatoes
½ cup fresh basil leaves
3 cloves garlic, crushed and peeled

¾ cup olive oil
¼ cup cider or white vinegar
2 Tablespoons sugar
2 teaspoons salt

*Put everything in the blender and blend well. Serving suggestions: on corn salads, lettuce and spinach or with crumbled feta cheese and garbanzo beans.*

## CUCUMBER SESAME

1 medium cucumber, peeled and cut in
  chunks (about 1 ½ cups)
3 cloves garlic, crushed and peeled
½ cup rice vinegar

¼ cup toasted sesame oil
2 Tablespoons sugar
1 ½ teaspoons salt

*Put everything in the blender and blend well. Serving suggestions: toss with rice noodles or quinoa and vegetables, use as a dressing for green bean salad or shredded carrots, beets, green onion and toasted sesame seeds.*

## PICKLED VINAIGRETTE

Don't throw that delicious pickle juice down the drain!

1 medium cucumber, peeled and cut in
  chunks (about 1 ½ cups)
½ cup parsley
4 cloves garlic, crushed and peeled
1 cup pickle juice, any kind

¾ cup olive oil
2 Tablespoons sugar (if using sweet pickle
  juice leave out the sugar)
1 teaspoon salt

*Put everything in the blender and blend well. Serving suggestions: lettuce salads, cucumber and tomato salads, green beans, pinto beans and sharp cheese, drizzle on top of your pork BBQ sandwich.*

## CUCUMBER QUESO

1 medium cucumber, peeled and cut in
   chunks (about 1 ½ cups)
8 ounces cream cheese
1 clove garlic, crushed and peeled

¼ cup freshly grated Parmesan or other
   aged hard cheese
1 teaspoon salt
1 jalapeño pepper (optional)

*Put everything in a food processor and blend well. Serving suggestions: toss with hot or cold pasta, top black bean cakes or corn muffins, dip tortilla chips, use as a pizza topping instead of tomato sauce, dip veggies in it.*

## RAITA

1 medium cucumber, zebra peeled, large
   seeds removed and grated (about 1 ½
   cups)
¼ cup plain Greek yogurt
1 Tablespoon chopped fresh mint leaves

1 clove garlic, minced
1 teaspoon sugar
¼ teaspoon salt
⅛ teaspoon cumin powder
Dash cayenne pepper

*Combine all ingredients in a bowl and mix well. Serving suggestions: Indian curry condiment, atop fritters, alongside any spicy meats like roast lamb or chicken, use as a dip for chips or crostini, top your shawarma.*

## TZATZIKI SAUCE

1 recipe Raita
½ cup crumbled feta cheese

SERVING SUGGESTIONS:
*with Falafel Spiced Green Bean Fritters, gyros, black bean cakes, on a platter with veggies, pita and hummus.*

---

### THICKENED CUCUMBER SAUCE

If you prefer a thicker queso, raita or tzatziki, you can squeeze out excess moisture from the cucumber by grating it and squeezing it gently to release some of the juice. Reserve the cucumber juice and combine with sparkling water for a refreshing drink and proceed with the recipe using the drained cucumber.

# Cucumber Salads

I don't love building cucumber trellises. But, if your cucumbers splay on the ground, all manner of wormy thing will eat them before you can say the word *salad*. I solved my trellis problem when I found an old fence gate on the side of the road one day. This gate turned trellis has enabled me to quadruple my cucumber production, which enables me to say salad a whole lot. Each salad serves four to six.

## CUCUMBER CHERRY TOMATO SALAD

4 medium cucumbers, zebra peeled and
  sliced (about 6 cups)
2 cups cherry tomatoes, sliced in half
½ cup fresh basil or parsley leaves, coarsely
  chopped

½ teaspoon salt
¾ cup Homegrown Herb Vinaigrette
  or Cucumber Tomato Basil dressing
  (see pages 43 and 115)

*Toss everything gently together in a bowl.*

## CUCUMBER RANCH SALAD

4 medium cucumbers, zebra peeled and
  sliced (about 6 cups)
¼ cup finely diced red onion
¼ cup fresh parsley leaves, chopped

¼ teaspoon salt
¾ cup Cucumber Buttermilk Ranch
  (see page 114) or your favorite
  ranch dressing

*Toss everything gently together in a bowl.*

## CUCUMBER ALMOND ARTICHOKE

4 medium cucumbers, zebra peeled and
  cubed (about 6 cups)
1 cup marinated artichoke hearts, quartered

½ cup roasted red peppers, diced
½ cup Pickled Vinaigrette (see page 115)
½ cup sliced almonds, toasted

*Toss everything gently together in a bowl.*

## CUCUMBER FETA CHICKPEA

4 medium cucumbers, zebra peeled and
cubed (about 6 cups)
1 (15-ounce) can chickpeas, drained and
rinsed
1 red bell pepper, diced

1 cup crumbled feta cheese
½ cup sliced Kalamata olives (optional)
¼ cup parsley leaves, chopped
¾ cup Cucumber Sesame dressing or
Pickled Vinaigrette (see page 115)

*Toss everything gently together in a bowl.*

## PICKLED CUCUMBER CARROT SALAD

4 medium cucumbers, zebra peeled and
cubed (about 6 cups)
2 cups shredded carrot
2 cloves garlic, minced
½ cup thinly sliced onion

¼ cup parsley leaves, finely chopped
1 cup cider vinegar
2 teaspoons salt
2 teaspoons sugar

*Toss everything gently together in a bowl. Allow to marinate 1 hour before serving.*

# Cucumber Cups with Black Bean Hummus or Pimento Cheese

Think of these sort of like deviled eggs. It's all about what you put into the center, and if your center is good then you will be happy and fulfilled. Pimento cheese is traditional and looks pretty, but I like to switch it up (see page 122). Makes 25–30 cups.

## CUPS

3–4 medium (2 ½–3 pounds) cucumbers
¾ cup pimento cheese or hummus

## BLACK BEAN HUMMUS

I (15-ounce) can black beans, rinsed and drained
2 Tablespoons vegetable or canola oil
I clove garlic, crushed and peeled

I teaspoon lime or lemon juice
¾ teaspoon salt
½ teaspoon chipotle pepper puree
¼ teaspoon cumin powder

*Blend all the hummus ingredients together in a blender or food processor.*

*Cut the cucumbers into I-inch-thick slices. Use a melon baller or a round teaspoon to scoop out the center of each slice, leaving a little bit of cucumber so there isn't a hole all the way through. Scoop your dip into the center of each cucumber slice and arrange on a platter.*

*If you are transporting these, wait to put the dip in until you get where you are going.*

## OTHER FILLINGS FOR CUCUMBER CUPS

Think of the cucumber as a vehicle for flavor!

- Garlic Herb Cream Cheese (see page 38)
- Smoky Pimento Cheese (see page 187)
- Sesame Green Bean Hummus (see page 138)
- Corn Chow Chow (see page 102)
- Sungold Tomato Pesto (see page 76)

# Chilled Cucumber Soup with Roasted Red Pepper Sauce

### SERVES 4–6

I think it is important for food to look pretty. Even in the most squalid places I've eaten (like out of a shared bowl on the Appalachian Trail in the rain), a little sprinkle of cinnamon or drizzle of balsamic brightens my outlook. Often those garnishes and flourishes are pretty tasty in and of themselves. In this case, the pepper sauce is as delicious as the soup, and the flavors complement each other. But you can get creative here. Cucumbers are a great canvas, so if you don't have peppers, sprinkle some chopped herbs on top, thin out a little pesto and drizzle that on top—heck, this soup is even good with a touch of Sriracha or berry BBQ sauce.

## SOUP

3–4 medium cucumbers, peeled and
   chunked (about 4 cups)
1 cup plain Greek yogurt
¼ cup sour cream or crème fraiche
¼ cup fresh herbs (basil, parsley, sage,
   dill, oregano, rosemary)

1 clove garlic, diced
1 Tablespoon honey
1 teaspoon salt

## ROASTED RED PEPPER SAUCE

½ cup roasted red peppers
2 Tablespoons extra virgin olive oil

1 clove garlic, diced
¼ teaspoon salt

*In a food processor or blender, combine soup ingredients and puree. Pour into a container and put in the fridge to chill.*

*Rinse out your blender and combine pepper sauce ingredients. Puree until smooth, adding a tiny bit more olive oil if needed.*

*Serve soup in individual bowls with the pepper puree drizzled in a pretty pattern on top, with bread, crackers or chips as a light lunch or as a first course to a late summer meal of Green Bean Cherry Tomato Salad, Corn on the Cob and Squash Casserole.*

# Easy Refrigerator Pickles

These are neither sweet nor sour pickles; they have dill in them but I wouldn't call them a dill pickle. What they are is crunchy and flavorful. Because there is no heat involved, they don't get soft like some canned pickles do. As a bonus, you can just keep adding cucumbers to the brine over several weeks for a continuous pickle supply. Makes about 2 quarts.

2 cups water
1½ cups sugar
3 cups cider vinegar
8 cloves garlic, peeled and sliced
10 bay leaves (fresh or dried)
2 Tablespoons fresh or dried dill
4 teaspoons salt
6 cups sliced cucumbers (3 pounds)

*In a sauce pot, bring the water and sugar to a boil; stir to dissolve sugar. Remove from heat, allow to cool 10 minutes and add vinegar. Add remaining ingredients, except cucumbers, to the brine.*

*Pack cucumbers in jars or whatever kind of container you like. Pour brine over cucumbers, making sure the brine is covering them. Put in the fridge and let sit at least 12 hours. Pickles will keep refrigerated for several months.*

*Serve as an appetizer with cheese, meat and other pickled vegetables, on sandwiches, chopped up in chow chow or topped with a bit of pimento cheese.*

# INTERVIEW WITH CHEF KAREN TAYLOR

Like so many kids whose parents own a business, Karen Taylor grew up in her family's restaurant business and pursued a different career when she had the chance but was lured back to working with food. As an account executive for Bell South in Atlanta, Karen loved to entertain and have friends over. Her friends kept telling her, "Your food is so good! You should be a caterer!"

Karen couldn't resist the pull of food praise and started a small catering business on the side. She jumped at the chance when offered a job helping to teach cooking classes with famous southern chefs like Paula Deen and Virginia Willis. Working with these folks, Karen saw new, exciting trends in the food industry as they were unfolding and learned skills that others might get from culinary school. "I wanted to go to Le Cordon Bleu and still work during the day, but they didn't have night classes so this was like going to school, but I was actually working."

When her parents moved to Southport, North Carolina, they encouraged Karen to move there and start a much-needed breakfast and lunch restaurant. Intrigued by the idea, Karen went to visit and, while chatting with the owners of a café, discovered the place was for sale. "One thing led to another, and now I'm actually doing what I love."

At Taylor Cuisine Café, Karen dishes up comfort food using collards, herbs, cucumbers and tomatoes grown in the garden in front of the restaurant. Farmers drive right up and invite her to choose from the fresh produce in the back of their trucks—they've learned that Karen will buy a few melons, bunches of crisp arugula, a bushel of ripe peaches—whatever is fresh and in season to incorporate into her inspired dishes. "Those peaches get cooked into all kinds of things, from a sauce accompanying pork, to cobblers and pies." Karen finds ways to use them all.

"Taste it, cook it, feel it and don't overthink it. The passion that you have for food, the receiver will taste it," she counsels when asked her philosophy. Her emphasis on simple, visceral pleasure in food comes through in the honest, evocative flavors that are the hallmarks of her dishes.

# Karen's Cucumber Gazpacho with Shrimp

1 pound fresh jumbo shrimp, peeled and
chopped
3 Tablespoons extra virgin olive oil
1 teaspoon kosher salt
1 teaspoon black pepper
½ teaspoon ground cumin
½ teaspoon paprika
2 large garlic cloves, finely diced

4 ripe Roma tomatoes, diced
3 large fresh cucumbers, seeded and diced
1 cup organic chicken broth (low sodium)
1 cup plain whole milk Greek yogurt
1 small red onion, diced
3 Tablespoons fresh lime juice
1 cup fresh cilantro, chopped
½ teaspoon cayenne

*Sauté chopped shrimp in olive oil, and season them with the salt, black pepper, cumin and paprika. Set them to the side to cool. In a food processor, add the rest of ingredients, blending until smooth. Then pour into bowl and add shrimp. Serve cold and garnish with fresh sprig of cilantro.*

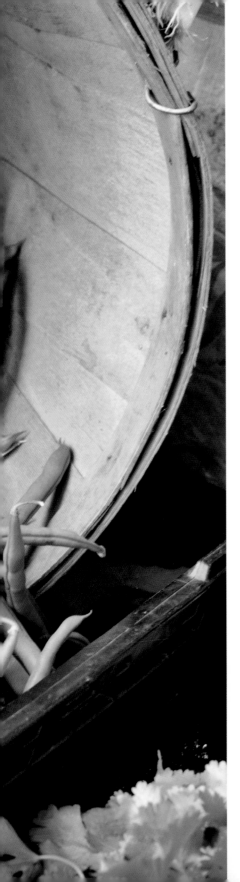

# 9

# Green Beans

To string or not to string, that is the question. Most folks these days don't really know the difference between all the old-time varieties of beans, but at least we all remember the stories of stringing beans on the porch. You know, the story of grandmas in flower prints and grandpas in overalls rocking in chairs with overflowing washbasins of beans. They chat with the neighbors or rock in time to the grandkid playing a fiddle, stringing beans all the while.

Unfortunately, for most, those days are long gone, along with our bean knowledge. As the famous seed saver Bill Best said, "Folks don't know beans about beans."

It is not surprising that commercial growers have made popular "string-less" bush varieties that are easier to pick and process; however, they are tough and have little flavor. The difference between those beans and an heirloom string bean is like the difference between instant coffee and a freshly made cappuccino. One is convenient and cheap; the other requires time and skill. Both have their place in the world, but one is tastier.

There are also a lot of varieties of beans that are more like French press coffee. They are string-less, sweet and tender, even if their flavor is not as complex as the heirloom bean. I highly recommend a French pole bean (growing up a pole as opposed to bush varieties) called Fortex. Prolific vines grow long, tender, flavorful beans.

Farmers' markets often have tender string-less beans for sale, and most farmers will let you taste one raw before you buy, but if you have a little time to sit on the porch and string some beans, I recommend trying some heirloom varieties.

Regardless of whether you choose to string or not to string, there are many ways to cook a bean. String beans are often better cooked long and slow, while those tender beans are perfect for salads. And if you happen to get a little tired of the traditional methods, try giving those beans a starring role in falafel or hummus.

## Falafel Spiced Green Bean Fritters

When I graduated from college with my art history degree, the only jobs I could find were picking up recycling and cooking at a Mediterranean deli. It wasn't what I expected, but I learned a lot from both experiences. I learned how to drive a big truck and that the trick to delicious falafel is to turn it green with lots of parsley. I use tough, end-of-summer green beans to make these in place of traditional chickpeas, but tender beans work just as well. The greener the better.

| | |
|---|---|
| 1 pound (4 cups) green beans | 3 Tablespoons cornstarch |
| 4 cloves garlic, crushed and peeled | 2 teaspoons lemon juice |
| ½ cup packed parsley leaves | 2 teaspoons cumin |
| 1 small onion, peeled and quartered (about ¾ cup) | 1 teaspoon coriander |
| | 1¼ teaspoons salt |
| 1 cup bread crumbs or cornbread crumbs | Oil for frying |

*Trim the ends off of beans and string if necessary. Bring about 6 cups of water to a boil in a good-sized pot. Add beans and simmer until tender (5–15 minutes depending on beans).*

*In a food processor, blend garlic until finely chopped. Add green beans, parsley and onion. Pulse until well chopped but not pureed. Add in remaining ingredients, except frying oil, and pulse to combine. If consistency is too loose to form patties, add another Tablespoon or two of cornstarch.*

*Heat a skillet to medium-high heat and add about 2 Tablespoons oil to coat. Spoon fritters (1–2 Tablespoons per fritter) into the pan and flatten slightly to spread. Flip after about 2–3 minutes and fry the other side. Makes 15–20 fritters.*

*Continue frying in batches, using additional oil as needed between batches. Alternatively, scoop fritters onto a greased sheet pan and bake at 350 for about 20 minutes, until firm. Serve with Cucumber Tzatziki Sauce and Herb Focaccia or Hoecakes, Roasted Red Pepper Sauce, Corn Chow Chow and Cucumber Salad.*

## Green Bean Salads

In the middle of summer, my salad greens are pretty sad. Dry, limp leaves bolt in the heat and turn bitter. Often I'm too busy picking green beans at that point to even notice, and fortunately, young tender green beans make beautiful salads. Their sweetness pairs well with lots of flavors, and most houseguests don't mind snapping beans in exchange for dinner. The following salad recipes serve 6.

### GREEN BEAN SALAD WITH CHERRY TOMATO AND FENNEL

2 pounds (8 cups) tender green beans,
    ends trimmed
2 cups cherry tomatoes, cut in half
2 cups basil leaves, finely chopped
¼ cup yellow fennel flowers or 1
    Tablespoon finely chopped fennel seed
½ cup fresh grated Asiago or
    Parmesan cheese
2 cloves garlic, finely diced

1 Tablespoon fresh lemon juice
3 Tablespoons extra virgin olive oil
1½ teaspoons salt

> ### WHAT THE HECK IS FENNEL POLLEN?
>
> Fennel pollen comes from this amazing yellow fennel flower that blooms right before the fennel plant starts setting seed. Some plants are bulb fennel, but some don't produce bulbs, instead making seeds prolifically. It is this seed fennel plant that produces little yellow flowers that are all flavor. Pick the tiny flowers whole and pop them in your mouth. The flavor is delicate fennel essence. After a few weeks, the fennel plants start to make seeds (which are also delicious), and the pollen is no more. The season is midsummer and it is fleeting, so enjoy it while you can.

*Bring about 3 quarts of water to a boil in a good-sized pot. Cut green beans into 2-inch lengths and cook for 5–8 minutes. They will still be a tad crunchy. Drain and run cool water over the beans. In a large bowl, combine beans with remaining ingredients. Serve at room temperature.*

## TOASTED PEANUT GREEN BEAN SALAD

2 pounds (8 cups) tender green beans,
  ends trimmed
1 ¼ cups toasted peanuts
¼ cup finely diced red onion
2 cloves garlic, finely diced

2 Tablespoons cider vinegar
1 Tablespoon sunflower or vegetable oil
2 teaspoons sugar
1 teaspoon salt

*Bring about 3 quarts of water to a boil in a good-sized pot. Cut green beans into 2-inch lengths and cook for 5–8 minutes. They will still be a tad crunchy. Drain and run cool water over the beans. Using a mortar and pestle, grind the nuts so that some of them are totally crushed but there are still some big chunks. You can do the same thing with a knife or food processor. Combine all of the ingredients in a pretty serving vessel (blue is a nice contrast to green), reserving a handful of peanuts to garnish the top of the dish. Mix well and sprinkle the reserved peanuts on top.*

## GINGER LIME GREEN BEAN SALAD

2 pounds (8 cups) tender green beans,
  ends trimmed
1 red bell pepper, finely diced
1 lime, finely grated, zest and juice
1 clove garlic, finely diced

1 Tablespoon grated or finely chopped
  ginger
1½ Tablespoons vegetable oil
1 teaspoon salt

*Bring about 3 quarts of water to a boil in a good-sized pot. Cook for 5-8 minutes. They will still be a tad crunchy. Drain and run cool water over the beans. Combine beans and remaining ingredients and toss gently to mix.*

# Slow Cooked String Beans with Bacon or Mushrooms

### SERVES 4–6

Oh my goodness, string beans are tasty! We grow Cherokee Trail of Tears beans, which can be eaten early in the summer as a fairly tender green bean; later in the summer they get stringy, and in the fall, the pods get tough and develop beautiful shiny black beans. At the stringy stage they are a little more work but worth it. I like to get everyone involved with bean making. While I'm frying up the bacon, I pass the beans to anyone with two hands for stringing.

4–5 slices bacon
1½ pounds (6 cups) string beans
3–4 cups water or stock

2 cloves garlic, thinly sliced
1 teaspoon salt
1 jalapeño, seeded and sliced (optional)

*Fry bacon in a heavy-bottomed sauce pan until golden brown and crispy. Meanwhile, remove stems and strings from beans. Remove bacon from the pot and add all remaining ingredients. Crumble bacon and add to the pot. Simmer for about 1 hour on low until beans are very tender.*

*Serve with Hoecake, Herb Focaccia or Bell Pepper Flatbread to soak up the cooking liquid. This is a great potluck item because it goes with anything.*

> ### MUSHROOM VERSION
>
> *Substitute 8 ounces mushrooms and 3 Tablespoons butter for the bacon. Slice and sauté mushrooms in the butter, until mushrooms are good and brown, add other ingredients and proceed with above recipe.*

## Dilly Beans

I was first introduced to dilly beans by a sister-in-law who was totally shocked that I had never had them. Apparently, some households have a jar of dilly beans in the fridge at all times. I try to make that happen in my household these days, because you never know when you are going to go on an impromptu picnic and need the tart crunch of a dilly bean to go with your cheese and bread or Bloody Mary. Makes 2 quarts.

2 pounds (8 cups) string-less green beans
3 ½ cups cider vinegar
3 cups water
2 teaspoons salt
4 cloves garlic, crushed and peeled
¼ cup fresh dill sprigs or 2 Tablespoons dill seed
2 teaspoons whole peppercorns

*Remove tops and ends of green beans, wash and divide evenly between two clean quart-sized mason jars. Bring cider vinegar, water and salt to a boil in a saucepan. Divide the garlic, dill and peppercorns evenly between the jars.*

*Pour the boiling liquid into the jars—making sure the liquid covers the beans. You can always top off the jars with a bit more vinegar. Put the lids on the jars and allow to cool on the counter.*

*Store the beans in the fridge—they will keep for several months. Alternatively, pack in sterilized jars and can in a boiling water bath for 15 minutes to make them shelf stable. Serve dilly beans in Bloody Marys, alongside sandwiches, as an appetizer with cheeses and meats or chopped up in salads.*

# Sesame Green Bean Hummus

I was at a potluck dinner party one summer evening, and the conversation turned to garden success stories. A friend was actually dismayed by the number of green beans she was picking every day. Her neighbor had kindly used his tractor to help plant the garden, and springtime enthusiasm had turned to summer stoicism as she felt compelled to waste not want not. She was sick to death of green bean salads, casseroles and sautés. I suggested this method for using up those plentiful green beans, and I thought she would kiss me. Sometimes all it takes is a new idea. Makes about 2 cups.

1 ¼ pounds (5 cups) green beans
¼ cup sesame tahini
2–3 Tablespoons toasted sesame oil
3 cloves garlic, crushed and peeled
2 teaspoons capers, pickled green beans
  or any savory pickle
1 teaspoon salt

*String beans if necessary and trim ends. Cook green beans in boiling water until very soft. Drain. Combine all ingredients in a food processor and process until smooth. Serve with tortilla chips, pretzels, cherry tomatoes, Hoecake or veggie sticks.*

---

### FREEZING GREEN BEANS

Do not attempt to freeze this hummus after it is made. The texture does not do well with freezing. However, you can use frozen green beans to make the hummus.

Freezing is a great way to preserve your green bean harvest. They have to be blanched or steamed before freezing, or pesky enzymes in the beans continue to break them down. Uncooked beans pulled out of the freezer will look like shriveled little green worms. To freeze: trim the ends and string if necessary, blanch for 1 or 2 minutes or steam for about 5 minutes, pack in plastic bags or freezer containers and freeze for up to one year.

# INTERVIEW WITH
# CHEF APRIL MOON HARPER

I met April in the early 2000s when she came to work at West End Bakery Café. Within her first week, she'd made the best chicken soup I'd ever tasted and whipped up cakes and pies faster than you could blink. It was obvious she knew her way around a kitchen, and unlike many accomplished chefs, she had serious baking skills.

Sometimes chefs travel a long way, growing and learning, to eventually come back to their roots. April Moon is one of those chefs. After finishing culinary school, she landed a job working as a chef for a computer company in Atlanta. The company had nine hundred employees and entertained lots of foreign clients. She was flown to New York to take pastry classes and San Francisco to learn to make dim sum and was mentored by chefs who taught her a huge variety of culinary techniques and traditions.

April ended up coming back to the mountains of North Carolina, where she had grown up with a very different type of food experience.

In her early years in Haywood County, everyone around her grew food and had community potlucks, where traditional southern dishes abounded. "There is a DNA to southern cuisine that I pull from because it's my comfort zone, but I also pull from other cuisines and experiences."

This is evident at her popular Sunny Point Café. To ease the wait customers readily endure most mornings, they can walk through the bountiful Sunny Point vegetable garden. April creates dishes that blend her experiences, like pasta carbonara with fresh green beans, duck eggs from her daughter's ducks and country ham instead of pancetta.

The garden at Sunny Point tells its own story. "It shows that sustainability is important to us as a restaurant," says April. "Kids who snack on green beans in the garden have ah-ha moments when they see those same green beans served." Growing much of her own food also enables April to infuse the dishes at Sunny Point with fresh flavors that reflect the journey from garden to plate.

## April's Mod Three-Bean Salad with Spicy Avocado Dressing

1 ½ pounds garden beans (yellow, purple, green and/or rattlesnake if you have them, any combination will work)

1 (15-ounce) can of black beans, rinsed and drained, or 1 ½ cups black beans

½ cup finely sliced red onion

2 garden tomatoes, cut into ½-inch chunks

2 ears fresh corn, shucked and roasted over open flame, then kernels cut off cob

4 ounces crumbled feta cheese

Spicy Avocado Dressing

Roasted and Toasted Pumpkin Seeds

*Tip and string fresh beans as necessary. Bring a large pot of salted water to a boil. Set up a large bowl of ice water next to the stove. Cook the beans in salted water until al dente, drain with a strainer and place them in the ice water to shock and preserve color and texture. Once cold, drain well, pat dry and place in a serving bowl.*

*Add the black beans to the garden beans in the serving bowl and toss to combine. Top beans with the finely sliced rings of red onion, diced garden tomato, roasted corn, feta cheese and Spicy Avocado Dressing just before serving. Garnish with Roasted and Toasted Pumpkin Seeds.*

## Spicy Avocado Dressing

I just ripe Hass avocado, split,
   seed removed and pulp scooped
   out with a spoon
¼ cup plain whole milk Greek yogurt
½ cup water
I lime, juiced
I clove garlic, minced

½ teaspoon salt
¼ cup olive oil
I fresh cayenne pepper, seeded and minced,
   or ¼ teaspoon dried cayenne pepper, to
   taste if heat is not your thing
I bunch fresh cilantro leaves, about I cup
   loosely packed

*Place all ingredients in a blender and puree until smooth. If not using immediately, cover lightly with wax paper or parchment to maintain color. If dressing seems too thick, it can be thinned with additional water added a few teaspoons at a time.*

## Roasted and Toasted Pumpkin Seeds

I cup hulled raw pumpkin seeds
½ teaspoon ground cayenne pepper
½ teaspoon chili powder
2 teaspoons ground cumin

¼ teaspoon ground cinnamon
½ teaspoon salt
I teaspoon canola oil

*Toss all ingredients in a bowl. Place a large sauté pan over medium heat. Add seeds and cook, stirring constantly until they begin to make a popping sound and smell delicious. Remove from heat and cool.*

# 10

## Summer Squash

I think I may have grown the world's largest zucchini. That was the summer I got my garden all planted, just in time to leave town for several weeks. Kind friends were put in charge of watering if it did not rain, and I hoped for the best. Well, rain it did—almost every day, in fact. My friends, who were also invited to pick ripe produce, didn't bother coming over much to check on things.

When I arrived home, my garden appeared to have quadrupled in size, and as I excitedly roamed around checking on things, I came upon a zucchini the size of a watermelon. Some folks would have tossed it in the compost or, at most, displayed it on the porch, but I brought my trophy inside to eat. Never one to waste food, I cooked up every bit of that squash and fed many a hungry mouth.

Summer squash is a most versatile vegetable. Unlike its cousin the cucumber, it can be baked, roasted, grilled and fried with great success. Water can be squeezed from it to incorporate into recipes where a dryer texture is required. Pickled or eaten raw it offers a nice crunch, and even its pretty flowers are tasty.

I have never understood the desire to unload homegrown summer squash on unsuspecting neighbors. I suppose I could grow enough to get tired of it, but as long as I have a freezer and can grate it up for winter casseroles, tortes and breads, it's hard to imagine.

My hope is that the following pages help the world find the key to unlimited squash potential.

# Flourless Chocolate Zucchini Torte with Chantilly Citrus Cream

I would not classify myself as a chocolate fanatic. My baker friend Tim is a chocolate fanatic. We used to start our workdays together at 3:00 a.m., and Tim would snack on chocolate chips all morning long. He regularly ate brownies for breakfast. That just won't work for me, unless we are talking about this torte. It is mind blowing. When it's in my house, I can think of nothing but its rich, fudgy, moist chocolate power. I have been known to eat it for breakfast. Makes one 10-inch torte or an 8-inch pan of brownies.

## TORTE

¾ cup cocoa powder

¼ cup cornstarch

¼ teaspoon baking soda

¼ teaspoon salt

1 stick (8 Tablespoons) butter, melted

1 cup semisweet chocolate chips

2 eggs

¾ cup sugar

1 cup pureed zucchini, about 2 small

2 teaspoons vanilla extract

½ cup chopped pecans, walnuts or hazelnuts

## CHANTILLY CITRUS CREAM

½ cup heavy cream

3 Tablespoons powdered sugar

1 Tablespoon orange zest

*Preheat oven to 350 degrees. In a large bowl, sift together the cocoa powder, cornstarch, soda and salt. Combine the melted butter and the chocolate chips. Chips will melt a bit, but it's fine if there are still some chunks. Add eggs, sugar, zucchini and vanilla and whisk well to combine. Combine with the dry ingredients.*

*Butter a 10-inch springform pan or tart pan and pour batter into the pan. Sprinkle chopped nuts on top. Bake for about 35 minutes, until torte is set in the middle. Cool completely and then refrigerate for 1 hour before serving. Warm torte is also good but will be hard to serve because it won't hold together.*

*Make Chantilly cream by combining heavy cream and powdered sugar; whisk until starting to thicken, add orange zest and whisk until just beginning to form peaks. Serve alongside torte.*

*Note: This can also be made as brownies in an 8-inch square pan—they will be thicker, so increase cooking time to 40 minutes. Cool and refrigerate at least 1 hour before serving.*

### Marinated Summer Salad

SERVES 6

Salads can be challenging. Especially if you take them to gatherings and forget the dressing. That is one of the many reasons I love a marinated salad. Made in advance and grabbed out of the fridge just before leaving, I never forget the dressing for this salad. The squash stays nice and crunchy for a couple of days, so leftovers can be taken to the next gathering, and no one is the wiser.

6 cups thinly sliced summer squash
1 red bell pepper, diced
¼ cup basil leaves, coarsely chopped
2 cloves garlic, minced or crushed

1 lemon, finely grated, zest and juice
⅓ cup extra virgin olive oil
1 teaspoon salt

*Combine all ingredients in a bowl and mix well. Refrigerate for at least 2 hours and up to 2 days. Serve alongside grilled burgers, chicken, Green Bean Cherry Tomato Salad, Herb Focaccia and Polenta Tomato Pie, on a bed of greens or tossed with cooked rice or pasta.*

# Fried Zucchini Pickles

County fairs are a big deal in our neck of the woods. Folks bring out their biggest pumpkins and prettiest pigs to show off, pies are judged and handmade patchwork quilts are on display. Fair food is almost always fried. These pickles remind me of fair food, but if I never end up frying them, they are just as good. Makes one quart of pickles or 3 cups fried pickles.

## PICKLES

1¼ cups cider vinegar

1 cup water

1½ teaspoons sugar

1 teaspoon salt

3½ cups zucchini, sliced ½ inch (about 2 medium)

3 cloves garlic, peeled and smashed

1 whole chili pepper

1 teaspoon mustard seed

1 teaspoon coriander seed

1 teaspoon black peppercorn

*Make at least 2 days before. Combine vinegar, water, sugar and salt in a quart jar or container. Stir or shake well until salt and sugar dissolve. Add all the remaining ingredients and refrigerate, covered, for at least 2 days and up to 2 months.*

## FOR FRYING

½ cup cornmeal

½ cup flour or cornstarch

1 teaspoon salt

Vegetable oil for frying

*Combine cornmeal, flour and salt in a bowl. Heat about ¼ inch of oil in a skillet until it starts to shimmer. Dredge pickle slices in cornmeal mixture and gently place in a single layer in the skillet. If the oil does not sizzle when you put the first pickle in, wait another minute before adding more pickles.*

*Fry for about 2 minutes on each side. Remove from the pan with a slotted spatula and drain on paper towels or clean newspaper. Add more oil as needed and continue to fry in batches. Serve alongside or inside burgers or sandwiches filled with cheeses, meats and veggies. Or serve up in a basket with ketchup or herb mayo for dipping.*

# Seared Summer Squash with Shrimp

SERVES 6–8

My husband grew up eating criminally overcooked summer squash. Scarred for life, he is now sensitive to any squash that even begins to be mushy. Seared squash gets a nice caramelized crust without the mushy texture. The trick is not overcrowding the pan. If squash gets packed in, the moisture will be released before it can sear and mushiness will ensue. With or without shrimp, I find even squash-sensitive folks like it seared.

4 medium zucchini, diced in 1-inch-square chunks (4 cups)

4 medium yellow squash, diced in 1-inch-square chunks (4 cups)

2 teaspoons salt, divided

4 teaspoons vegetable or olive oil

1 pound small shrimp, peeled and deveined (optional)

1 red bell pepper, finely diced

1 cup diced green onions

½ cup basil leaves, sliced

2–3 cloves garlic, finely diced

1 lemon, finely grated, zest and juice

*In a bowl, combine squashes and 1 teaspoon of salt. Get a skillet searing hot. You will be cooking the squash in about 3 batches depending on the size of your skillet. Add about a teaspoon of oil to the skillet and 1 layer of squash. (Lift the squash out of any water that has rendered in the bottom of your bowl.)*

*Do not stir. Cook for about 2 minutes and then flip the squash and sear about 2 more minutes, transferring to a bowl. Continue searing squash in batches, adding oil to the pan between each batch.*

*If using shrimp, add 1 teaspoon oil to the pan. Sear shrimp, stirring constantly for about 1 minute, until all shrimp is pink. Add shrimp to the bowl with the seared squash. Gently toss with remaining teaspoon of salt and remaining ingredients.*

*Serve as a main dish over pasta or rice or a side dish alongside Ricotta Grits Soufflé, Green Bean Fritters, Toasted Peanut Green Bean Salad, Herb Focaccia, Peach and Tomato Salad or Corn Salad.*

## *Pan Fried Stuffed Squash Blossoms*

In the case of squash flowers, the males are often disappointing. Looking at my blossom-covered plants from afar, I assume many young fruits are on the way, only to discover, on closer inspection, that many of the flowers are male. They are the ones that shoot out first on a long, stiff stem, only to wilt fruitless. They sometimes manage to pollinate a hardworking female flower, proving their occasional usefulness. But I like to pluck those macho blossoms and make them useful by stuffing and eating them. I don't recommend doing that with any other variety of male, but in this case you will not be disappointed. Makes 10.

2–4 ounces goat cheese
1 clove garlic, finely diced
1 Tablespoon chopped rosemary, parsley,
   chive or dill

10 large, mostly closed squash blossoms
1–2 Tablespoons butter

*Combine goat cheese with garlic and herbs in a bowl. Gently peel back one or two petals of each squash blossom and place a spoonful of goat cheese inside, dividing goat cheese between the blossoms. You may need more or less depending on size of blossoms. Fold the petals back over the goat cheese. Heat a skillet on medium heat and melt 1 Tablespoon of butter. Fry blossoms in 2 batches, about 1 minute on each side. Add more butter to the skillet if necessary in between batches.*

   *Serve as an elegant appetizer or alongside Seared Summer Squash with Shrimp, cucumber salads, Savory Tomato Cobbler, Green Bean and Cherry Tomato Salad, garlicky chicken or Chilled Cucumber Soup.*

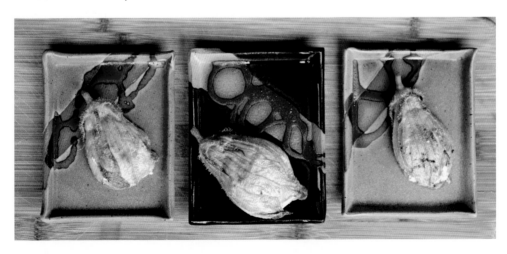

# Grilling Summer Squash and Fresh Herb Remoulade

SERVES 4–6

Believe it or not, there is a right way to do this and a wrong way. I have definitely done it the wrong way and speak from experience when I say this: Do not overcook your grilled squash! Sometimes I get distracted, which was the case when friends arrived for dinner the day I marinated squash in a pesto sauce and grilled the heck out of it. Squishy, ugly squash was the result. I learned the hard way to keep it simple, hot and quick.

## FRESH HERB REMOULADE

4 cups herb leaves (parsley, basil, cilantro, dill and so forth)
1 lemon, juice and zest

4 cloves garlic, crushed and peeled
⅓ cup mayonnaise
½ teaspoon salt

## SQUASH

2 pounds squash: pattypan, zucchini, yellow squash and so on
1 Tablespoon extra virgin olive oil
1 teaspoon salt

Freshly ground black pepper
1–2 Tablespoons fresh or dried herbs (optional)

*If using remoulade, make it first by combining all ingredients in a food processor or use a mortar and pestle and process until smooth. Set aside.*

*For the squash, preheat grill to medium high or about 400 degrees. If using pattypan squash, cut in thick wedges; otherwise, cut squash in half lengthwise. Make a crosshatch pattern in the flesh so spices can penetrate and squash will cook more evenly. Coat evenly with olive oil, salt and pepper. Dip an old (but clean) towel in vegetable oil and, using tongs, grease the grill grates. Put squash directly on grill grates and grill 2–3 minutes on each side until grill marks appear on flesh.*

*Remove to a platter and sprinkle with fresh herbs if using or serve alongside Fresh Herb Remoulade, Sungold Tomato Pesto, garlic butter, Corn Chow Chow, sautéed mushrooms or crumbled bacon.*

# HUGE SUMMER SQUASH CARE AND USAGE

There comes a time in every cook's life when you hit the big time. Big time zucchini, that is. Whether you grow it yourself or it is left in your care, big zucchini are a boon to some and a burden to others. I personally love them, because it's a ton of food all at once and, if treated with care, can make for some delicious victuals. Now any variety of summer squash can get quite large and be used in the following applications. I focus on zucchini, because they are the ones that hide under the squash leaves, while other varieties find it harder to hide because of their yellow, orange or white skin tones. It pays to be green.

## INITIAL CARE

If your zucchini is more than two feet long, you may want to peel some of the tough outer skin off and remove some of the seeds. Cut off the ends and cut it in half lengthwise. If it seems that the outer skin is very thick, use a vegetable peeler to peel off the outer layer. If the seeds inside seem big and tough, use a spoon to scoop some of them out. If you don't get them all, it is okay. Most seeds will get tender when cooked, and you probably won't be able to tell they are there.

## GRATE IT UP

If you have a food processor, this is a good time to dust off that grater attachment and put it to good use. If not, a box grater will do the trick. Using the coarse holes on the grater, grate all the zucchini and remove any large, tough seeds that pop up.

### Freezing

You can use grated zucchini right away or you can put it in plastic bags and freeze it. It will keep for four to five months in the freezer. If you get one in July, it is perfect for making squash casserole at Thanksgiving. An August windfall will make your December holiday zucchini bread.

### Thawing for Use

When you thaw zucchini, the water will separate from the flesh. This can be perfect if you were planning to squeeze the water out of your squash anyway. For example, squash casseroles (see page 154) call for squeezing out excess water before mixing into batter. If your recipe does not call for squeezing out excess moisture, mix the water that separates into whatever it is you are making.

### Slice It and Dice It

You may prefer to slice or dice your squash. That will work just fine, but it is not the best technique to use if you plan to freeze it. I like to quarter a big one lengthwise, slice it into pie shapes and make zucchini pickles. If you freeze sliced squash, it is best to grill it or sauté it first; otherwise, it will be rubbery when thawed.

# Squash Casseroles

I get lots of folks to help me out in the kitchen. Sometimes kids wander in and ask what they can do, and if I have squash in my fridge, I put them to work grating it up. It's a pretty safe job and hard to mess up—although I did discover that it's helpful to tell them which size holes to use on the grater. My friend Bailey used the smallest holes once and we ended up with squash mush. Use the big holes. It's quicker and a bit more appetizing.

## CASSEROLE BASE

5 cups grated summer squash
4 eggs
1 cup grated Cheddar or
  Monterey Jack cheese

2–3 cloves garlic, finely diced
2 teaspoons dried or fresh herbs
  (sage, oregano, basil, thyme)
½ teaspoon salt

## TOPPING

1 ½ cups bread crumbs, crumbled tortilla chips or cracker crumbs
½ cup grated cheese

## OPTIONAL ADDITIONS

1 cup diced bell pepper
1 cup cooked and crumbled sausage
4–5 slices cooked and crumbled bacon
½ cup caramelized onion
1 cup corn kernels

½ cup sautéed mushrooms
1 cup finely chopped kale, Swiss chard
  or spinach
1 finely diced jalapeño or chili pepper

*Preheat oven to 350 degrees. Put squash in a strainer in the sink and squeeze dry. If using frozen squash, simply thaw and strain from liquid that separates when thawed. Combine all casserole ingredients and any desired add-ins and put in a buttered 2-quart casserole dish. Combine topping ingredients and sprinkle on top. Bake for 20–25 minutes until firm in the center. Serve with Tomato Plates, Slow Cooked String Beans and Bacon, Corn on the Cob, Cucumber Salads, Mashed Sweet Potatoes or Mixed Greens with Roasted Butternut.*

# · AUTUMN ·

# 11

## *Paw Paw*

In our neck of the woods, we can get a little taste of tropical flavor with the miraculous paw paw. These strange-looking fruits, native to the eastern United States, grow on trees and are the largest edible fruit indigenous to this area. Not only do they survive, they also thrive without much care. Legend has it that Lewis and Clark would have perished on their expedition if these sticky sweet, banana-like fruits had not sustained them through areas where other food was scarce.

A paw paw looks sort of like a discolored, mangled mango. When ripe, they are greenish yellow with brown spots and have a scent reminiscent of bananas forgotten in a hot car on a sunny summer day. Cut open, the flesh is securely attached to multiple dark brown seeds the size of lima beans. A paw paw doesn't last long and needs to be processed within two or three days of harvest to avoid the rotting flesh smell they emit when overripe. Maybe this is why we don't see them in grocery stores?

Never mind all that. Hidden inside these fruits is the most exotic flavor you can experience in a plant native to North Carolina. A cross between banana, mango, pineapple, passion fruit and citrus, paw paw flesh is divine if treated properly.

Try substituting paw paw for banana in smoothies or mango in salads, salsas and sauces, or try some of the recipes that follow. Whatever way you choose to enjoy paw paw, know that you are supporting a native plant, tropical in flavor but lacking the long transportation times (and high carbon footprint) of most tropical flavors.

---

### HOW TO EAT A PAW PAW

First, peel off the skin and remove the seeds using your hands or a food mill. This is a tedious process that you'll want to set aside some time for. Even using a food mill takes a while to separate all the seeds from the flesh. You can put the seed-free pulp in plastic bags or containers and freeze it for up to two years. I freeze paw paw flesh in one-cup portions so I can pull it out and make paw paw ice cream for a taste of the tropics in the doldrums of winter.

If you don't want to fuss with processing all that pulp, you can simply eat the paw paw flesh and spit out the seeds. It is delightful like that too. Whatever you do, be careful with cooking paw paw. Something strange (and unpleasant) happens to the flavor when raised to higher temperatures. It is possible to cover the odd flavor with lemon and spices, but considering how difficult they are to process, I want to taste paw paw. Meringue cookies work because they are baked at a low temperature, which preserves the magical flavor.

---

## Paw Paw Ice Cream

Indulging myself with good books is a guilty pleasure. I joined two book clubs, so I feel like my books are assignments. Not only do I feel less guilty about curling up with a good book, but I also have the added pleasure of gatherings to discuss the merits of characters while eating food inspired by the story. I made this ice cream after reading *Asfidity and Mad-Stones* by Byron Ballard. The book is a tale of wisdom from the hollers of Appalachia. Sweet, tropical-tasting paw paw fruits sustained folks living in hardscrabble nooks and crannies of southern Appalachia, and ice cream is the wisest way to show off its luscious flavor. So says my book club.

| | |
|---|---|
| 1 cup pureed paw paw | 1 cup sugar |
| 1 cup heavy cream | ½ teaspoon salt |
| 1 cup half-and-half | |

*Combine all the ingredients in a bowl. Stir well. Freeze in your ice cream freezer according to its instructions. Serve alongside pound cake, sugar cookies or all by its lonesome. Makes 1 quart.*

# Paw Paw Salsa

When traveling in Ghana, I walked past many a loaded mango tree planted in front yards, along sidewalks, by secluded streams and in the middle of the bush. I was envious because in the West African climate, these highly sought-after fruits grew seemingly anywhere without much fuss. Really, there is no need to be envious, because in our region we have paw paws. Mango salsa move over. Makes 2½ cups.

1–2 jalapeños or hot peppers
2–3 cloves garlic, crushed and peeled
2½ cups coarsely chopped tomatoes or
  cherry tomatoes

I cup paw paw flesh
¼ cup cilantro leaves
I teaspoon salt

*Cut peppers in half lengthwise and remove seeds. Put hot peppers and garlic in the bowl of a food processor and blend until finely chopped. Alternatively, chop finely with a knife. Add all other ingredients and pulse a few times to chop. Or finely dice tomatoes, paw paw, cilantro and mix everything well. Serve with chips, on tacos or roast chicken, alongside Sweet Potato Peanut Stew or Carolina Red Rice, in a pulled pork sandwich or eat with a spoon.*

## Meringue Cookies with Paw Paw

This is the only way I like to bake paw paws. If this delicate fruit gets overheated, it doesn't act quite right. As a delicate person, I can relate. The low heat required for these cookies is just enough to make them crispy and bring out the amazing tropical flavor of paw paw. Makes 35 to 40 cookies.

2 egg whites (save yolks for Fingerprint Jam
   Cookies, page 62)
⅓ cup granulated sugar
⅓ cup powdered sugar, sifted
2 Tablespoons paw paw puree

*Preheat oven to 225 degrees. In the bowl of an electric mixer, beat egg whites on high until soft peaks form. Beat in granulated sugar 1 Tablespoon at a time. Beat in powdered sugar. Fold in paw paw puree. Scoop about 1 Tablespoon at a time onto a parchment-lined baking sheet or use a piping bag to pipe onto parchment. Put them fairly close together; they don't expand much, if at all.*

*Bake for 1 hour. Turn oven off and allow to sit in closed oven for 1 more hour to continue to dry out. Cool and then store in airtight containers at room temperature for up to 1 week. Serve as a light, refreshing dessert after a brunch or with a cup of afternoon tea. These add a welcome zing to a Christmas cookie selection.*

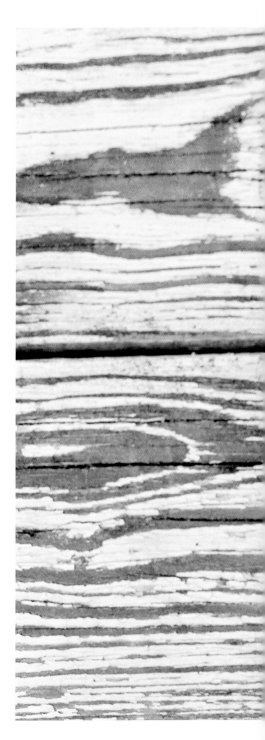

Author photo.

# 12

## *Apples*

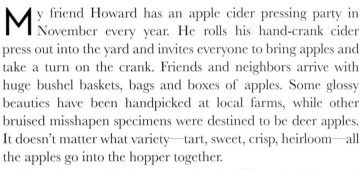

My friend Howard has an apple cider pressing party in November every year. He rolls his hand-crank cider press out into the yard and invites everyone to bring apples and take a turn on the crank. Friends and neighbors arrive with huge bushel baskets, bags and boxes of apples. Some glossy beauties have been handpicked at local farms, while other bruised misshapen specimens were destined to be deer apples. It doesn't matter what variety—tart, sweet, crisp, heirloom—all the apples go into the hopper together.

He sets it up perfectly, encouraging the kids to do all the work while the adults supervise. The fresh-pressed juice is a complex, sweet elixir that is the essence of apple flavor. Batch after batch go into bottles, jugs and jars for guests to take home. Kids drink hot cider, adults sip on hard cider made from last year's juice and sometimes a bit of apple moonshine is passed around. Apple treats abound: caramel dipped, baked, slaws, dried, sauced and doughnut stuffed. The apple is the star of the show.

This gathering is one of the many reasons I love apple season. There are few foods as versatile and adaptable. Apples eaten out of hand are a quick, satisfying snack; baked into cakes and pies they are comfort food; in salads they offer tart crunch; combined with meats, grains or pureed into sauce, apples can be consumed multiple ways and multiple times a day. The following pages contain some of my favorite ways to eat my daily apple.

# Lemon Arugula Apple Radish Salad

If I could have one garden wish granted, I would wish for a prolific lemon tree growing in my yard. There is nothing out there with the same juicy brightness as a lemon. Until I get old and move to South Georgia, I will have to make do with lemon balm, lemon verbena, lemon basil and a few precious lemons from the store.

## SALAD

6 cups arugula leaves
2 cups radish leaves, or some other leafy
    green
4–8 radishes, sliced
1 medium apple, sliced

## DRESSING

1 lemon, finely grated zest and juice
2 Tablespoons extra virgin olive oil
2 cloves garlic, minced
1 Tablespoon sugar
¼ teaspoon salt

*Combine salad ingredients in a bowl. Whisk together dressing ingredients. Just before serving, toss the salad with the dressing. Serve this salad as a light lunch with Sweet Potato Cornbread on the side or alongside a mushroom green onion omelet, Bell Pepper Flatbread, Pepper Hazelnut Salad with Orange and Fig, Winter Squash Soup or Spinach and Sorghum Meatloaf.*

# Chicken Salads with Apple

I use any excuse to turn the oven on when it starts to get cold outside. Roast chicken seems like as good an excuse as any. Roast chicken season seems to coincide with apple season, which also coincides with party season (and of course you can use a store-bought rotisserie chicken). These chicken salads have a little sweetness to them from the apples and are often the first thing to run out on the buffet table. It's always nice to be the person who brought the most popular item! Serve along with crackers or crostini, in tiny sandwiches or wrapped up in lettuce leaves. The following each make about 5 cups.

## APPLE FENNEL AND DRIED CHERRY CHICKEN SALAD

3 cups diced cooked chicken

2 cups diced apple (1 large)

1 cup finely diced fennel bulb,
   tender stem or frond

¾ cup diced dried cherries, cranberries
   or raisins

### DRESSING

⅓ cup cider vinegar

⅓ cup extra virgin olive oil

2 cloves garlic, finely diced

2 Tablespoons sugar

½ teaspoon salt

½ teaspoon Dijon or brown mustard

2–3 Tablespoons mayonnaise (optional)

*Put salad ingredients in a bowl. Blend dressing ingredients in a blender or whisk together in another bowl. Combine dressing with chicken mixture and mix well. Taste and add up to ½ teaspoon more salt if needed. Allow chicken to absorb dressing (refrigerated) for 1 hour before serving. Toss well and serve.*

## APPLE GOAT CHEESE PECAN CHICKEN SALAD

3 cups diced cooked chicken
2 cups diced apple (1 large)
¼ cup chopped parsley leaves
3 ounces goat cheese, crumbled

½ cup toasted pecans, chopped
Dressing listed above or ¾ cup good
   Italian vinaigrette

*Combine all ingredients in a bowl and toss well. Taste and add up to ½ teaspoon more salt if needed. Allow chicken to absorb dressing (refrigerated) for 1 hour before serving. Toss well and serve.*

# Bacon Apple Beef Burgers

There is an old apple tree on the edge of the woods near our farmhouse. No one knows the variety, but the small gnarled apples taste tart and crisp. When we discovered the tree, it hadn't been trimmed in years, so the wild branches held apples so high in the air we had to climb a tall ladder to pick. We don't get many, and they are hard to process, but they inspired me to combine them with beef and bacon, and I will be forever thankful to that old apple tree.

1 pound ground beef
1½ cups peeled and finely minced apple
   (2 small)

2 slices thick-cut raw bacon, diced
1 teaspoon salt
Fresh ground pepper to taste

*Prepare grill or stovetop griddle. In a large bowl, combine all ingredients and mix. Patty out burgers, pressing fairly flat (makes 4–5, burgers will shrink when grilled). Sear burgers on high heat on each side for 1 minute. Move burgers to cooler part of grill and grill to desired doneness. Serve with buns, mustard, pickled onions, pickled collards and sweet potato fries. Or crumble and serve on top of a salad with arugula, chopped red cabbage, toasted pecans and a warm bacon vinaigrette.*

# Apple Slaws

Have you ever listened to *Splendid Table*? It's a foodie radio show, and sometimes people call in to play "Stump the Cook." They describe 5 things in their fridge, and the cook has to come up with a dish that uses all 5 ingredients; she wins if the dish tastes good. Sometimes I play that game with myself when I make slaw. Here are a couple of winners. Each serves 6–8.

## APPLE FENNEL COLESLAW

6 cups sliced or shredded cabbage

3 cups thinly sliced apple (2 medium)

1 large fennel bulb, thinly sliced

½ cup coarsely chopped green fennel fronds

½ cup sliced green onions

3 Tablespoons cider vinegar

½ cup sour cream or mayonnaise

1 teaspoon salt

*Put all ingredients in a bowl and toss well to mix. Allow to sit at least 10 minutes before serving for flavors to meld. Serve with Hoecakes, thinly sliced ham and ginger tea for a perfect lunch.*

## APPLE CIDER MUSTARD COLESLAW

6 cups sliced or shredded cabbage

3 cups thinly sliced apple (2 medium)

½ cup sliced green onion tops

¾ cup fresh apple cider

4 cloves garlic, finely diced

2 Tablespoons Dijon or brown mustard

2 teaspoons mayonnaise

½ teaspoon salt

*Put all ingredients in a bowl and toss well to mix. Allow to sit at least 10 minutes before serving for flavors to meld. Toss again just before serving. Serve with Bacon Apple Beef Burgers, Sweet Potato Cornbread, Velvety Mac and Cheese, Squash Casserole or Bell Pepper Flatbread.*

# Apple Chips

MAKES 2-3 CUPS

Years ago, my friend Barbara showed me mason jars full of dried apples lined up on shelves in her sunny kitchen. They weren't leathery and soft but crunchy like a potato chip. Sweet and satisfying, not to mention kind of healthy, I figured out why she had so many—I could eat a jar by myself. She used a food dehydrator, and I did for a long time, but to get them really crunchy takes almost two days. Recently, I wanted apple chips to serve with a cheese platter and discovered my stash almost gone. I tried them in the oven, and not only was it faster, but the apples got even crispier. My husband, Reid, likes them naked, but it's easy to sprinkle them with spices for a variety of flavors.

5–6 medium apples

OPTIONAL ADDITIONS

Cinnamon
Sugar
Ginger
Nutmeg
Curry Powder
Chinese 5 Spice Powder

*Preheat oven to 200 degrees. Peel apples and slice very thinly—about $1/16$ inch thick. Spread apple slices on top of cooling racks and then put cooling racks on rimmed baking pans. Sprinkle apples with a thin layer of optional additions and put into the oven for 2–3 hours, depending on the juiciness of your apples.*

*To test for crunchiness, take 1 apple slice out of the oven and allow to come to room temperature, 2–3 minutes. Break in half or taste to see if they are crunchy. Apples will keep for up to a year in tightly sealed jars or bags.*

*Serve with cheeses, nuts and dips, on top of salads, crumbled with popcorn and caramel or just munch as a snack.*

# Apple Crisps and Crumbles

When the first apples of the season start coming in, my mouth starts watering for apple crisp. It's simple to make, and the hot apples with the crispy top taste exactly like fall should. Then after about the third batch, I want something different. Here's the lucky part: there are endless variations on this theme! Try some of my suggestions (pages 174–75) or add your own twist.

## BASIC APPLE CRISP FILLING

6 cups peeled and sliced apples (4 medium)
½ cup sugar
1 teaspoon cinnamon
2 Tablespoons cornstarch
¼ teaspoon salt

## TOPPING

½ cup all-purpose flour
½ cup oats
½ cup sugar
4 Tablespoons butter, cut in about 10 pieces

*Preheat oven to 350 degrees. In a bowl, mix apples, sugar, cinnamon, cornstarch and salt. Transfer apples to a 9-inch deep-dish pie pan or oven-safe baking dish. Using the same bowl, mix flour, oats, sugar and butter. Use your fingers to rub together until nice and crumbly. Spread crumble on top of apples. Put your pie dish on a baking sheet (in case it bubbles over). Bake for about 50 minutes until edges are bubbly and crumble is golden brown on top.*

## CARAMEL APPLE CRISP

*Substitute this sauce for sugar and cinnamon in apples:*

4 Tablespoons melted butter          ½ cup heavy cream
1 cup packed brown sugar             1 teaspoon vanilla extract

*Combine in a saucepan, bring to a boil and cook on medium low for 5 minutes. In a bowl, combine apples, salt and cornstarch and mix well. Add cooked caramel sauce to apples and proceed with above recipe.*


## GINGER CRISP

*Add to apples:*
   ½ cup chopped crystalized ginger


## CRANBERRY CITRUS

*Add to apples:*
   ¾ cup dried or fresh cranberries, chopped
   ½ cup orange juice
   1 teaspoon finely grated orange or lemon zest


## ALMOND PLUM

*Add:*
   1 cup chopped dried plums (prunes)—to apples
   1 cup sliced almonds—to topping


## BUTTERSCOTCH

*Add to apples:*
   ¾ cup butterscotch chips

## BERRY

*Add to apples:*
   1 ½ cups frozen blueberries, blackberries, raspberries or mulberries

## BROWN SUGAR PECAN

*Add to topping:*
   1 cup pecan pieces
   ½ cup brown sugar

## CUSTARD APPLE

*Substitute:*
   1 (14-ounce) can sweetened condensed milk for sugar in apple mixture

*Add:*
   1 egg, whisked, to apples

## CHOCOLATE SPICE

*Add to apples:*
   ¼ teaspoon ginger
   ¼ teaspoon nutmeg
   ¼ teaspoon cardamom
   ¼ teaspoon cloves

*Add to topping:*
   ¾ cup chocolate chips

# Apple Gingerbread Pound Cake

### MAKES 1 BUNDT CAKE

My husband's Aunt Bill was a notorious baker. I never got to meet Aunt Bill, but she lives on through her "secret family recipes." Her coconut cake is heaven on earth, but unfortunately, I am forbidden to share the recipe. I will have to be satisfied with sharing a completely altered version of her pound cake. Bill's recipe included Crisco and margarine but no apples, spices or molasses. I did have a copy of her recipe sitting on my counter as I came up with this one, but since I changed almost everything, I'm hoping I won't get in trouble.

3 cups peeled and coarsely chopped apples
   (2 medium)
2½ sticks butter (1¼ cups)
1 cup sugar
1 cup packed brown sugar
⅓ cup sorghum or light molasses
⅓ cup milk
Finely grated zest of ½ a lemon
1 Tablespoon finely grated fresh ginger

4 eggs
3 cups all-purpose flour
1 teaspoon baking powder
½ teaspoon salt
1½ teaspoons powdered ginger
1 teaspoon cinnamon
¼ teaspoon nutmeg
¼ teaspoon cloves

*Preheat oven to 325 degrees. Use a food processor or a knife to very finely chop the apples. In a mixer, cream the butter and sugars. Add molasses, milk, lemon zest and ginger and mix well. Scrape down sides of the bowl; add in eggs and beat well. Add in apples.*

*Sift together dry ingredients and fold into wet ingredients. Generously butter a bundt pan and pour the batter in. Bake for 60–70 minutes, until toothpick inserted in the center of the cake comes out clean. Serve with Ginger Lemon Whipped Cream.*

## GINGER LEMON WHIPPED CREAM

1 cup heavy whipping cream
¼ cup powdered sugar
Finely grated zest of ½ a lemon
1 teaspoon finely grated fresh ginger

*Combine cream and sugar and whip until soft peaks form. Add in the lemon zest and ginger.*

# INTERVIEW WITH CHEF JOHN FLEER

John Fleer loves the game of soccer. Faithfully sporting his trademark red Adidas Gazelle tennis shoes, he spent several years volunteering as a coach, hoping to inspire kids to love the game as much as he does. Apparently, he was successful; a good friend of mine now coaches soccer in red tennis shoes as homage to John, his first soccer coach. John's enthusiasm for soccer has proven almost as contagious as his enthusiasm for food. Longtime head chef at the celebrated Blackberry Farm in Tennessee, John now owns and operates Rhubarb and The Rhu in Asheville, North Carolina, where he inspires that same love of fresh, heartfelt, artfully crafted food in his guests.

That food love had an early start. Growing up visiting his grandparents in the Tidewater area of Virginia, John spent weeks at a time crabbing in the bay and helping harvest veggies from their huge garden. "My grandparents weren't extraordinary cooks, but the food was extraordinary because it was all out of the garden."

A semester in Venice brought about the revelation that in other cultures, food was not merely functional. "I was astounded by the amount of energy spent on what would be eaten, who was invited and what the occasion would be." John began cooking for small groups of fellow students and inviting Italian students to come and share their traditions. He shopped in the street markets and started building his skills.

Years later, John cites these experiences as inspiration, noting that one of the most important things he learned was a deep respect for tradition. "It is advisable and best to cook what you know," he muses, and growing up in the southern culinary tradition means he begins there. But when it really starts to get interesting for him is when that southern food is exposed to other ethnic or geographic influences. "What happens when you push a tradition to evolve? What about mouthwatering corn pudding with chilies or Indian spices?"

Using his "mental taste buds," John makes lists of ingredients and draws lines between things he'd like to use together. These lists are ever-changing and dependent on what is in season, what is fresh and what needs to be used. He recommends tasting food in raw form "to know where it started" and to continue to taste it all along the way to understand the transformation. John contends, "You won't know how you transformed something if you only taste the end product. The difference between following a recipe and cooking is making an effort to understand how you are transforming those ingredients."

# 13

## Peppers

I was fascinated to find out (embarrassingly) late in life that the pepper plant originated in the Americas. Mexico is its native ground. Peppers feature heavily in Central American cuisine, so that makes sense. What shocked me was the relatively recent introduction of peppers to the rest of the world. While I think of Asian and African cuisines as being dominated by the spicy sweet tang of chilies, those continents did not see this plant until the sixteenth century.

When this came into my consciousness, I was being schooled by someone twenty years my junior while eating a colorful, highly seasoned stew in West Africa. Ground peppers made the base for the stew while chunks of pepper mixed with goat and peanut in the broth. Everyone around us was eating similar dishes, and pepper plants were growing out of every crevice where there was a spot of soil. It was hard to imagine this food culture shifting and embracing peppers in such an all-encompassing way just a few centuries ago. What had they eaten before this plant gave them fire in the belly?

This moment was yet another reminder that food and culture are always evolving and changing. Many of our food traditions are only a few generations old, and although we can mourn the loss when a tradition falls out of favor, it makes way for something new. Right now, new traditions are being born, and I like to imagine a day when people gather around tables piled with freshly roasted vegetables that they have recently plucked from the garden and kids snack on strips of pickled bell pepper instead of french fries. It's happening in some places already. Who knows, maybe in another three or four hundred years our food culture will have evolved to the point that people will be shocked to find out early twenty-first-century Americans didn't eat salad every day.

# Bell Pepper Flatbread

There is nothing I like better than a big ol' pile of peppers—all colors, shapes and sizes. I could gaze at them for a good long time, but sometimes because I like looking at them so much I let them get a little older than is ideal. In my efforts to honor their colorful beauty, I wait for the perfect dish to come along where they will be the star of the show. Pepper flatbread is that dish. The color and flavor of the peppers preserved and intensified makes me glad I waited.

## FLATBREAD DOUGH

2 cups warm water

1 Tablespoon yeast

1 Tablespoon sugar

1 Tablespoon salt

1 Tablespoon olive oil

2 cups all-purpose flour

2 cups whole wheat bread flour

*Combine all ingredients in the bowl of a stand mixer or a large bowl. Use the paddle attachment on the mixer and stir on low for about 5 minutes or use your hand to mix ingredients in the bowl for 5–10 minutes. Dough will not be very firm. Cover and allow to rise for 1 hour—it should double in size.*

## ADD

4 cups diced bell pepper, all different colors
   (4+ peppers)

1 cup grated sharp Cheddar (optional)

2 Tablespoons chopped rosemary or basil
   leaves (1 Tablespoon dry)

1 teaspoon garlic powder

*Mix in these ingredients and allow to rise for 1 more hour.*

## ASSEMBLY

*Preheat the oven to 400 degrees. Place a 17x13 sheet pan in the oven for about 5 minutes to preheat. Remove from oven and spread 1 Tablespoon olive oil in the pan. Using a rubber spatula and working quickly, scrape the risen dough in the hot pan and spread with spatula into a rectangle. It's OK if it doesn't get to all the corners.*

*Bake for 45–55 minutes. It will be well browned on top. Remove from the oven and allow to cool about 5 minutes before removing from the pan and cutting. Serve alongside salads and soups or cut in half horizontally and toast to make sandwiches. Keep leftovers in the fridge; slices will toast beautifully for several days.*

# GRILLED OR ROASTED PEPPERS

At the neighborhood tailgate market one August afternoon, with piles of multicolored peppers in numerous variety all around, I asked my farmer friend how she liked to cook her gorgeous peppers. She replied she only ever grilled them. I was surprised, because with peppers abounding, I assumed she would get tired of the same old thing. But after some thought, I realized grilled and roasted peppers were my favorite and actually incredibly versatile. Once cooked, they can go on top of or into anything. I even think they would work on ice cream.

*Author photo.*

## GRILLING PEPPERS

*If grilling small peppers, put them in a lightly greased grill wok or a cast-iron skillet. Heat grill to medium high or about 400 degrees. If your peppers are large, dip an old towel in vegetable oil and, using tongs, grease the grill grates. Put large peppers directly on the grill grates. Grill 5–10 minutes, flipping every couple of minutes until all sides have grill marks and are starting to blister. Remove and let peppers cool 5–10 minutes or serve whole right away. If you wish to remove the skins, peel off starting in the blistered areas. Pull peppers apart with your hands and remove stems and seeds. (Use gloves if you are seeding spicy peppers.)*

## ROASTING PEPPERS

*Preheat oven to 400 degrees. Lightly oil a sheet pan and spread peppers in the pan so that they are not touching each other. Roast 10–20 minutes, flipping after about 5 minutes, until peppers are starting to brown and blister. Follow earlier instructions for skinning and seeding.*

## USES FOR GRILLED AND ROASTED PEPPERS

IN: salads, soups, sauces, pimento cheese, salsas, biscuits, cornbread, butter.
ON TOP OF: meat, fish, tempeh, burgers, sandwiches, roasted winter squash, beans, potatoes, vanilla ice cream?

# Roasted Pepper Hazelnut Rice Salad with Orange and Fig

SERVES 6

I know fall has arrived when I have all the ingredients on hand to make this salad. The bell peppers have ripened, showing off their colors; fresh figs and nuts are falling off trees; and the first citrus fruits of the year have begun to appear from warmer climates. I put them all together to celebrate the season.

4 cups cooked rice

1½ cups grilled or roasted bell peppers, sliced into 1-inch pieces

1 cup green onion tops, sliced

½ cup toasted hazelnuts or chestnuts, chopped

½ cup diced fresh figs

1 medium orange, finely grated, zest and juice

1 teaspoon salt

1 teaspoon sugar

*Combine ingredients in a bowl and gently toss to combine. Serve alongside roasted meat, baked sweet potatoes, meatballs, brussels sprouts, winter squash casserole, cider-braised collards, Gorgonzola cheese toast, Bacon Apple Beef Burgers, Lemon Arugula Apple Salad or pot roast.*

## COOKING PERFECT RICE

You can use this method for any type of rice. I heard about doing it this way from *America's Test Kitchen*, and it really works. You basically cook it like most people cook pasta. Get a good amount of water in a good-sized sauce pot, bring it to a boil, add your rice to the boiling water, bring back to a boil and simmer for 12–40 minutes depending on if you are cooking white, brown, short- or long-grain rice. Taste a grain of rice, and if it is your desired doneness, drain the rice using a fine mesh sieve. Put it immediately back in the pot with the lid on if you want to keep it warm. Fluff gently with a fork before serving. It is that simple!

*For 4 cups cooked white rice:*

6 cups water

1¾ cups long-grain white rice

*Simmer for about 12 minutes, check for doneness and drain.*

# Roasted Red or Green Pepper Sauce

At the end of harvest season, right before first frost, I have piles of multicolored peppers. They look beautiful together, but in the case of sauce, I like to sort them by color. If they are all blended together, the resulting sauce is an ugly brownish color. Also, the colored ones are so much sweeter—they want to shine in recipes like this. Absolutely, make Green Pepper Sauce, too, just do it with some parsley to brighten it up and give it an extra depth of flavor that is wonderful in its own way.

## BRIGHT-COLORED PEPPER SAUCE

1–2 cloves garlic, peeled
1 teaspoon fresh lemon juice
1 cup grilled or roasted brightly
   colored peppers

¼ cup extra virgin olive oil
½ teaspoon salt

*Combine garlic and lemon juice in food processor or blender. Add remaining ingredients and puree. Serve as a garnish for soups, Roasted Root Vegetables or roasted chicken; on top of pasta, rice or polenta; or use as a spread for crackers, chips and cheeses. Will keep in the refrigerator for several weeks.*

## ROASTED GREEN PEPPER SAUCE

*Substitute green peppers and add:*
   1 cup packed parsley leaves to sauce

# Homegrown Smoky Pimento Cheese

Pimento cheese is like a rainbow. There is a full spectrum of colors, varieties and flavors. I grew up hating pimento cheese because it was the mass-produced grocery store variety. Homemade pimento cheese is on the other end of the spectrum. Take this metaphor a step further, and homegrown pimento cheese is like ultraviolet light in the rainbow. It is so amazingly delicious, it disappears.

You can use jarred peppers from the store and it will still be delicious, but if you want to experience ultra pimento cheese, try growing the peppers.

1 cup roasted pimento or red bell peppers, diced

2 cups grated sharp Cheddar cheese

1 cup grated smoked Gouda or smoked provolone cheese

8 ounces cream cheese, room temperature

2–3 cloves garlic, finely diced

1–2 jalapeño peppers, finely diced (optional)

¼ cup mayonnaise

½ teaspoon smoked sea salt

½ teaspoon smoked paprika

*Combine all ingredients in a bowl and mix well. You can even put on gloves and mix with your hands if that is easier. Use to make grilled pimento cheese sandwiches, stir into grits, serve on top of sliced tomatoes or pickles, alongside Grilled Summer Squash or with lots of other dips, so that when it disappears there is still something to eat. Makes 3 cups.*

## Sriracha Style Chile Garlic Sauce

I often let my hot peppers stay on the plants until they ripen to red. They have a sweeter flavor, perfect for sauce. I've always made hot sauce, but my neighbor Eric was telling me about his homemade version of Sriracha sauce, which is made with red jalapeño peppers. This recipe was inspired by that conversation and is my new favorite. It's a tad more garlicky than Sriracha, but totally addictive.

12 red jalapeños, about 3 cups
8 cloves garlic, crushed and peeled
⅓–½ cup cider vinegar
4 teaspoons sugar
2 teaspoons salt

*Wearing gloves, cut jalapeños in half; remove seeds and stems. Rinse in a colander to remove any remaining seeds. Put all ingredients in a blender (start with ⅓ cup vinegar and add more if you like a thinner hot sauce) or food processor and puree until smooth. Transfer to a saucepan, bring to a boil and simmer 2-3 minutes.*

*Put in a glass jar in the fridge. Sauce will keep in the fridge forever. Alternatively, put sauce in sterilized canning jars and can them in a boiling water bath for 10 minutes for a shelf-stable sauce. Keep in the fridge after opening jars.*

NOTE: If you desire an extra smooth consistency in your hot sauce, remove skins by boiling whole peppers in water 5–10 minutes. Drain and cool. Wearing gloves, peel skin off of peppers, remove seeds and stems and proceed with recipe. Makes 1½ cups.

## Chile Garlic Black Bean Coconut Spread

I like to find ways to wash fewer dishes, and this is often what I make in the food processor after a batch of Chile Garlic Sauce. I don't clean it one bit in between. No need to measure precisely, I just leave about a Tablespoon of sauce in the bottom, add the other ingredients and then clean the food processor with tortilla chips and my mouth. Of course, you can put the sauce on anything from Bacon Apple Beef Burgers to Fried Zucchini Pickles, but these spreads are a delicious way to clean the food processor.

I Tablespoon Chile Garlic Sauce
I (15-ounce) can black beans, drained

¼–⅓ cup canned coconut milk
¼ teaspoon salt

*Puree ingredients together in blender or food processor, starting with ¼ cup of coconut milk and adding more for your desired consistency.*

## Red Pepper Sriracha Hummus

I cup roasted or grilled sweet red peppers
I (15-ounce) can garbanzo beans, drained
  (or I ½ cups cooked beans)
¼ cup extra virgin olive oil
I clove garlic, crushed and peeled

I Tablespoon lime juice
2 teaspoons Sriracha or homemade
  Chile Garlic Sauce
½ teaspoon salt

*Combine all ingredients in the bowl of a food processor. Process until very smooth and creamy. Serve with tortilla chips, pretzels or crostini or use on a sandwich as a condiment with pickles, cheese and spinach.*

## Pickled Green Pepper Strips

Big Jim Peppers are the ones I usually use for this. They are long and pointy with a bit of spicy heat. You can use bell peppers, and if you like a little heat, throw in a chile or two. I like to make them just before first frost when I'm cleaning off my pepper plants at the end of the season. Makes 1 quart.

3–4 cups sliced green pepper
   strips
2 cloves garlic, peeled
1¾ cups cider vinegar
1¼ cups water
3 Tablespoons sugar
1 Tablespoon mustard seeds
1 Tablespoon coriander seeds
1½ teaspoons salt

*Pack the peppers in a clean quart-sized canning jar. In a sauce pot, bring all the other ingredients to a boil. Pour boiling mixture over the peppers and screw on the lid immediately. Let jar cool, and for safety's sake, keep peppers in the fridge. They should be sealed and will stay good for up to a year, even after opening. Let peppers pickle for at least 3 days before serving. Serve in Bloody Marys, on grilled pimento cheese sandwiches or as a condiment alongside Squash Casserole, Green Bean Fritters, Collards with Beans, Roasted Root Veggies, Greens and Eggs or Carolina Red Rice.*

# · WINTER ·

14

## Winter Greens

When the snow is falling on the hoop houses outside the kitchen window, I sip hot tea and hope my hearty winter collards, kale, chard and spinach will survive the winter weather. Mostly, they do survive, and I am rewarded for covering them with plastic and ground cloths, because the cold gives them a sweetness I've never tasted in pre-bagged grocery store greens.

I feel lucky that in North Carolina I can grow food in my yard all year round. When I open the refrigerator and realize I have put off going to the grocery store one too many days and no veggies are in the crisper drawer save an onion, my garden comes to the rescue.

That onion gets put to good use chopped up and slow cooked with beans and collards, and I can put off going to the grocery store another day.

# Spinach and Sorghum Meatloaf

SERVES 6

The first time my (very grown up–seeming) nephew Patrick made me dinner, it was meatloaf. He made it Italian style with provolone and soppressata sausage mixed in. Oh my, did he impress his proud aunty! Meatloaf has always been peasant food, scraps of meat held together with bread and eggs and mixed with flavorful spices. Folks added whatever they had on hand as flavorful fillers. In Italy, it was bits of sausage and cheese, but in my house, it's greens. This Appalachian take on the traditional dish uses sorghum and spinach to round out the flavor and impress health-conscious diners.

2 teaspoons bacon grease or extra virgin olive oil

6 cups (8 ounces) packed spinach or Swiss chard leaves

1¼ teaspoons salt, divided

1 pound lean ground beef

1 cup bread crumbs

2 eggs

2 cloves garlic, finely diced

2 Tablespoons sorghum or light molasses

1 Tablespoon dried or fresh chopped oregano

¼ cup fresh grated Parmesan cheese (optional)

*Preheat oven to 350 degrees. Heat the oil in a skillet and coarsely chop the greens. Sauté greens with ¼ teaspoon salt on high heat for about a minute until wilted. Let greens cool. In a bowl, combine all remaining ingredients and mix well. Mix in greens. Put in a greased 9x5 loaf pan or shape into a free-form loaf on a greased sheet pan. Bake for 40–45 minutes. Allow to sit for a couple of minutes before slicing with a serrated knife.*

*Serve alongside Roasted Carrots with Herb Aioli, Lemon Apple Arugula Salad, Corn Salad, Marinated Dill Potato Salad, Bell Pepper Flatbread, Potatoes and Brown Butter or baked sweet potatoes.*

NOTE: This meatloaf is also delicious with hearty greens, such as collard greens or kale. Chop them very fine and sauté for 5–10 minutes before adding to meatloaf.

## *Collards with Ham or Beans*

SERVES 12–14

My vegetarian dad pretty much always cooks a ham for Christmas dinner. Guess which lucky girl gets to take the ham bone home most years? It is perfect timing, because you must eat collard greens on New Year's Day, and ham stock makes them even more meltingly delicious. Now, having said that, beans are a great stand-in for a ham bone if your vegetarian dad is coming for dinner.

### COLLARDS IN HAM STOCK

1 large ham bone with bits of meat still
   attached
4–6 quarts water
2 bunches (3 pounds) collard greens

3 cups diced onions (2 medium)
1 Tablespoon cider vinegar
1 teaspoon salt, extra to taste

## Optional Additions

Hot sauce
2–3 cups canned tomatoes
1 cup apple cider
1 cup raisins
6 cloves garlic, sliced
Cooked bacon or sausage

---

### COOKING COLLARD GREENS

Collards are often much thicker and tougher than other greens. Swiss chard melts into tenderness when it is sautéed, but collards need a bit more time and effort to achieve their full tender potential. As with most things, it is worth the effort. A well-cooked pot of collards is one of the most satisfying, nourishing foods imaginable. The other benefit is you have this amazing cooking liquid called pot liquor or "potlikker" that you can slurp or crumble cornbread into. Potlikker will cure what ails you!

---

*In a 10- to 12-quart pot, combine the ham bone and water and simmer, covered, 3–8 hours. (This is a perfect thing to do atop a woodstove.) You may need to add more water if you choose to do a longer cooking time. Remove the bone from the pot, making sure any meat bits stay in the pot.*

*Wash collards well and cut off tough stems that extend below the leaf. Coarsely chop remaining leaves. Add collards, onion, vinegar and salt to ham stock along with any optional additions. Simmer for at least 45 minutes. Use a slotted spoon to dish out the collards onto plate or serve in bowls with the pot liquor and sweet potato cornbread for crumbling into it.*

NOTE: This recipe does make a large batch that works well for New Year's Day revelries, but leftovers freeze great.

## VEGETARIAN COLLARDS WITH RED BEANS

10 cups water
2 cups dried kidney or pinto beans
2 teaspoons salt
1 large bunch (1½ pounds) collards
1½ cups diced onion (1 medium)

2 Tablespoons extra virgin olive oil
1 Tablespoon cider vinegar
1½ teaspoons fresh ground black pepper
2 teaspoons smoked paprika
Hot sauce to taste

*Combine water, beans and salt in a large pot and bring to a slow simmer. Simmer, covered, 1 hour. Wash collards well and cut off stems that extend below the leaf. Coarsely chop remaining leaves. Add collards and remaining ingredients to the pot and simmer covered 1 more hour or until beans are tender. Check occasionally and add a bit more water if needed to keep the beans covered in liquid.*

## Pickled Collards

As the story goes, the more collards you eat on New Year's Day, the more money you will have in the coming year. Well, I try to eat my collards on the right day, but on January 2, collard greens go on super sale at all the markets. That is when I go collard crazy, bringing home huge bags of the thick hearty leaves and spending hours making pint after pint of these delicious pickles. When I look at all my jars stacked up together, it feels like money in the bank.

8 cups packed (12 ounces) sliced collard
  greens
2 cups thinly sliced onion (1 large)
1 cup diced carrot or red pepper (optional)
3 cups water

1 ½ cups cider vinegar
1 Tablespoon mustard seeds
2 teaspoons salt
1 teaspoon coriander seeds
½ teaspoon fennel seeds (optional)

*Combine all ingredients in a large pot and bring to a boil. Simmer, stirring occasionally, for 3–5 minutes. Pack in sterilized jars and can in a boiling water bath 15 minutes. Jars that have been canned will keep unopened for a year in a cool, dark place. Alternatively, skip the canning process and keep in the fridge for up to 6 months.*

*Use as a sandwich garnish with meats, cheeses, eggs or roasted vegetables. Serve alongside squash pie, Hoecakes, Bacon Apple Beef Burgers, Mustard Dill Potato Salad, Green Bean Fritters or Potato Mushroom Custard Pie. Put in tacos or sandwiches or chop pickled collards and combine with fresh ginger and hot sauce for a delicious side dish.*

### DON'T THROW OUT THE PICKLE JUICE!

I never throw out pickle juice and especially not collard pickle juice. It makes the very best salad dressing. The garlic and the parsley are nice, but simply blended with olive oil I love to drizzle this on vegetables from asparagus to zucchini.

1 cup collard pickle juice
¾ cup extra virgin olive oil

½ cup parsley leaves
2 cloves garlic, crushed and peeled

*Blend together.*

# Making Sauerkraut

It might sound strange, but uncooked fermented foods have great bacteria that's good for the gut. My tummy hurts sometimes, and my digestion feels sluggish. When that happens, I reach for something fermented. Instead of buying expensive probiotic pills, I eat kraut. It's hard to find uncooked sauerkraut at the grocery store. It's usually canned, which kills all the good bacteria, but it's really easy to make, not to mention fashionable. So not only will your tummy feel good, but your homemade kraut will also make you feel hip.

*Author photo.*

6 cups unchlorinated or filtered water
¼ cup kosher or non-iodized salt
1½–2 pounds fresh cabbage, green or red

*Bring 2 cups of water to a boil and stir in the salt until dissolved. Add remaining 4 cups cold water to the brine solution to cool. Slice cabbage into bite-sized pieces and put about half of it into a very clean jar or crock that you can fit your whole hand into. It needs to hold at least half a gallon. Pour about 3 cups of brine into the jar with cabbage. Use a very clean hand to squeeze the cabbage with the brine—this releases juices and breaks down cell walls. Do this for several minutes so that cabbage is noticeably softer. Add more cabbage and more brine, stopping 3–4 inches from the top of the jar. Repeat the squeezing process with the new cabbage.*

*Fill a quart- or pint-sized plastic bag with the remaining brine, zip it shut and stick it in the jar—this will weigh down the cabbage so it stays submerged. If the bag leaks, it will not dilute the brine. Cabbage must stay submerged in brine to properly ferment.*

*Put the lid on and set jar on your counter with a rag under it in case it leaks. Keep the temp between 60 and 75 degrees for 3 weeks, taste and, if it is krauty enough, refrigerate. If you like a stronger flavor, leave out for another week or so.*

*If your kraut turns a strange color or gets super soft and slimy, something went wrong and you will have to ditch it; however, if a little white bloom forms on top of your brine while fermenting, this is totally normal—just use a clean spoon to skim it off.*

*Enjoy kraut as an appetizer alongside Smoky Pimento Cheese and hummus or on sandwiches, salads and bratwurst.*

# INTERVIEW WITH CHEF KEITH RHODES

Keith Rhodes doesn't even need to be asked about his family's culinary heritage. It is woven into him and seems to flow out of him as he talks, like part of his body and soul. He has taken that deep knowledge of foodways, traveled with it, improved upon it and made it his livelihood. As owner and chef of Catch restaurant in Wilmington, North Carolina, he shares his deep history with sustainably caught seafood dishes and fresh, inspired vegetable pairings.

Keith's mother died when he was young, which meant that Keith split his time between his maternal and paternal grandparents. In one home, he was vegetarian, as his mother's parents were Seventh-day Adventists. At his other grandparents' house, there was a huge garden that his granddad tended. As soon as Keith was "old enough to see over the stove," he was involved in the food preparation.

"I used to always watch my grandad cook. One of the things I would watch him do was segmented grapefruit with sugar on top, roasted under the broiler." His granddad had worked on the railroad and brought home creative preparations. He also worked as a bartender and caterer at parties in some of Wilmington's affluent white homes. Keith got to tag along and was inspired by the amazing black cooks working behind the scenes. They used a variety of spices, good cuts of meat and seafood to make top-notch, traditional southern dishes. "The party atmosphere was electric; the cooks were making prime rib, beef tenderloin, crab dip and pimento cheese. I saw how that made people happy, and it was very inspiring. As a youth it attracted me."

Keith draws on all of these experiences as well as his travel experiences to share with the rest of us his own inspired, creative dishes. His infectious love of food is apparent as he describes the smell of fresh-harvested slices of cucumber or the feel of peach fuzz on the tongue. He talks about grilled asparagus and okra with reverence: "When you grill okra, it's a whole different ballgame. You might not think you like okra until you've had it grilled—a little bit of olive oil, salt and pepper on a hot grill—it is absolutely delightful."

Keith's passion for good food doesn't stop at his restaurant. Keith shares his appreciation for fresh food with kids in the community outreach that he does. "We go out to the low-income housing projects and we plant gardens out there; we go back, harvest those foods and show kids and parents how to make something right there." He likes to share with people "the knowledge of how fresh food can better your whole diet and mind's state."

When it comes to bringing out the best flavors in fresh foods, Keith makes it sound so simple. "Little enhancements can really bring out personality." Olive oil, lemon, sea salt, pepper and basil are his five ingredients that work magic. He suggests trying them on just about anything, including corn, tomatoes, lettuces—even slices of orange.

Love of food and the desire to share it seem to be his other magic ingredients, and his food is infused with all of the above.

## Keith's North Carolina Sweet Potato Salad

4 ounces sweet potato, peeled, cut into
  1-inch chunks
¼ cup cranberries
¼ cup hot water

¼ cup St. Germaine
4 ounces spinach leaves
¼ cup crumbled goat cheese
1 teaspoon shelled hemp seeds

*Parboil the sweet potato until fork tender, drain and cool in fridge. Meanwhile, rehydrate cranberries in equal parts hot water and St. Germaine. Let sit for 1 hour, drain and reserve. Heat a nonstick medium sauté pan on medium heat, add 1 Tablespoon of extra virgin olive oil and sauté cooked sweet potatoes until lightly browned. Divide spinach into 2 bowls; add cooked sweet potatoes between the two salads. Sprinkle each salad with half of the cranberries, goat cheese and hemp seeds and drizzle with 2 Tablespoons Honey Shallot Dressing.*

## Keith's Honey Shallot Dressing

½ cup sliced shallots
1 cup soybean oil
⅓ cup honey
1 Tablespoon Dijon mustard

1 teaspoon dried thyme
1 teaspoon black pepper
1 teaspoon kosher salt
⅓ cup seasoned rice wine vinegar

*Roast shallots in sauté pan with oil on low heat for 30 minutes, until golden brown. Remove from heat and let stand for 1 hour. Add shallots and remaining ingredients to a tall quart-size container and blend with stick blender or in blender until smooth.*

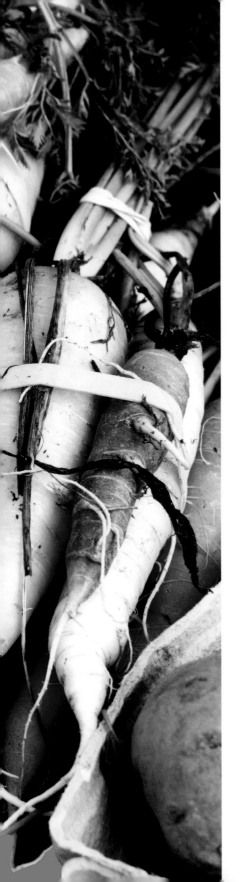

# 15

## Root Vegetables

I love to dig potatoes with kids. It is like a treasure hunt. The plant marks the spot; digging down through the dirt you come upon FOOD! Just like buried treasure, potatoes and other root vegetables hide their glories underground. Kids find it especially wondrous that unassuming green plants reveal golden globes of potatoes, ruby-colored radishes, garnet carrots and opal turnips. As the harvest basket fills, the excitement grows, with kids hollering, "I found another one!"

The treasure of root vegetables isn't over once the harvest basket is full. In addition to the roots themselves, many of the greens are edible and delicious (potatoes being an exception). In most cases, roots can be stored outside of the refrigerator for weeks or even months, to be enjoyed in the darker days of winter. Baked, boiled, roasted, whipped, candied, fried, grated, fermented, marinated, sautéed and raw, it's almost impossible to grow tired of these vegetables because there are endless ways to prepare them.

Whether you dig them out of the dirt or get your root veggies somewhere else, these recipes are designed to keep you warm and satisfied through the colder months of the year.

## Roasted Potatoes on Rosemary Skewers

SERVES 6

You know I'm havin' a fancy party when I trim up the rosemary bush. I once had a ten-year-old plant that took up half a vegetable garden bed. After that experience, I learned to plant rosemary in the flower bed because if it takes over the flower bed I can still eat. No matter where I plant, I look forward to doing a big trimming a couple times a year so I can make these skewers. They are elegant and simple, which is not my usual style, but every once in a while I like to have a fancy party.

2 pounds small fresh potatoes
1 Tablespoon extra virgin olive oil

1 teaspoon salt
10–15 (4-inch-long) sturdy rosemary stalks

*Preheat oven to 350 degrees. Toss potatoes with olive oil and salt on a sheet pan. Roast potatoes 30–35 minutes, until they are tender. Let potatoes cool for a few minutes, then use a metal skewer or chopstick to put a hole all the way through the center of each potato. String the potatoes on the rosemary skewers.*

*Serve warm or at room temperature as an appetizer or alongside roasted chicken, braised pork, Spinach and Sorghum Meatloaf, Bacon Apple Beef Burgers, Greens and Eggs or a simple supper of sliced apples and cheeses.*

# Spicy Pickled Onions

Pepe, a friend who grew up in Mexico, told me how to make this amazing relish. We cooked together for years, exchanging ideas and tips and discussing what we were going to make for dinner when we got home from cooking at work. He grew up eating lots of spicy peppers, and when I had a multitude of habaneros, he suggested this trick. The vinegar and the salt tone down the heat of the peppers a bit and season the onions perfectly.

3–4 habanero peppers (or 10 jalapeños)
3 cups very thinly sliced onion
1½ cups rice vinegar
1 Tablespoon fresh lime juice
1 teaspoon oregano
1 teaspoon salt

Combine all the ingredients in a glass quart jar and mix well, making sure the onions are submerged in liquid.

Refrigerate for at least 24 hours. Relish will keep in the fridge forever. Serve it with pulled pork, in tacos, on roasted winter squash, as garnish for potato soup, in nachos, on any kind of sandwich or as a condiment on your Bloody Mary bar.

# Whole Roasted Carrots with Garlic and Herb Aioli

### SERVES 4

As the days cool off, I begin to harvest the carrots that have spent the summer underground. Some summers they get more attention than others, and sometimes they are a bit thin and maybe even a touch bitter from their long, hard life underground. I get it; I would be thin and bitter if I never saw daylight. Roasting the carrots sweetens them right up, and a slather of aioli makes them downright elegant.

## AIOLI

1 large head of garlic
2 cups parsley, cilantro or even chickweed
¼ cup extra virgin olive oil

1 Tablespoon fresh lemon juice
¼–½ teaspoon salt

## CARROTS

1 Tablespoon butter
1 pound peeled carrots (long, thin ones work best)
½ teaspoon salt

*Preheat oven to 400 degrees. Wrap garlic in aluminum foil and put into the preheating oven. Bake for about 35–40 minutes—garlic cloves should be quite soft when pressed on. When the oven is up to temperature, put butter on a sheet pan and put in the oven for 1 minute to melt. Toss carrots with melted butter and salt on the sheet pan. Roast carrots for about 20 minutes, until slightly brown and blistered.*

*Allow garlic cloves to cool slightly before handling. Peel or squeeze out the cloves and put in a blender or food processor with aioli ingredients. Blend until smooth and creamy.*

*Serve carrots on a platter at room temperature with aioli drizzled on top or on the side for dipping. Serve as an appetizer or alongside roasted meats, Potato Mushroom Custard Pie or Roasted Potatoes on Rosemary Skewers.*

# Whipped Potatoes with Carrots and Brown Butter

SERVES 6

The first time I had brown butter, I thought it was a complex sauce concocted with a multitude of rich, unbelievably delicious ingredients. Sometimes it's the simple things that make all the difference. In this case, it is very simple. Brown butter is nothing more than caramelized butter, and if caramel sauce was savory, this is what it would taste like. Potatoes are good with straight-up butter, but they are amazing with brown butter.

6 cups (2 pounds) peeled chunks of potato
1 cup peeled diced carrot
4 Tablespoons butter

¼ cup milk, half-and-half or almond milk
1½ teaspoons salt
Fresh ground pepper to taste

*Combine potatoes and carrots in a pot and cover with water. Bring to a boil and simmer, covered, for 15–20 minutes until quite tender. Meanwhile, in a saucepan, melt the butter and cook on low for about 5–8 minutes, until butter is a caramel color and solids form on the bottom of the pan.*

*Reserve 1 cup of the cooking water and drain the potatoes. Combine the veggies, reserved water, milk, salt and pepper. Using electric beaters or an immersion blender, whip these together until fluffy (or mash with a potato masher). Drizzle the brown butter over the potatoes just before serving or put the brown butter in a little pitcher and serve with potatoes at the table. Serve alongside green bean casserole, Pan Seared Winter Squash with Cider and Greens, roasted meats, coleslaw or black-eyed peas.*

# Potato Mushroom Custard Pie

SERVES 4

Warm winter comfort food like this is best served at a table with low light and funky music playing. This pie puts me in the mood to do indoor things like reading magazines and drinking wine, taking a warm bath, knitting with the ladies, circling things I want to grow in the seed catalogue and occasionally playing Twister.

2 cups peeled and diced potatoes
1 Tablespoon vegetable oil
1 ½ cups sliced mushrooms
1 ½ cups diced yellow onion (1 medium)

½ teaspoon salt
1 Tablespoon chopped fresh sage leaves
  (2 teaspoons dried)
1 clove garlic, very finely diced

## CUSTARD

6 eggs
½ cup grated Asiago or Gruyère cheese
3 Tablespoons plain Greek yogurt, sour cream or ricotta cheese
½ teaspoon salt

*Preheat oven to 350 degrees. Put potatoes in a sauce pot, cover with water and bring to a boil; cook for 5–7 minutes until tender and drain well. Heat a 10-inch oven-proof skillet over high heat and add the oil, mushrooms, onion and salt. Turn to medium heat and sauté for about 10 minutes, until mushrooms and onions are soft.*

*Meanwhile, whisk together the custard ingredients in a bowl. Add the cooked potato, sage and garlic to the skillet and stir. Pour custard evenly over the veggies and put in the oven. Bake for 25 minutes, until the center of the pie is set. Slice into wedges and serve warm alongside Herb Focaccia, cider-braised collards, sweet potato oven fries, Apple Coleslaw, Slow Cooked Green Beans and Bacon or Mixed Greens with Roasted Butternut Salad.*

NOTE: If you don't have an oven-proof skillet, this can be made in a 9-inch deep-dish pie pan. Put the potato mixture in a greased pie pan and pour the custard over it. Increase baking time 30–35 minutes.

NOTE 2: Use leftover cooked potatoes. If you have leftover baked, boiled or roasted potatoes, this is a great way to use them up.

# HOW TO ROAST ROOT VEGETABLES

When I was in college, I attempted to make roasted vegetables for a potluck, and they turned out more like steamed veggies than roasted ones. I had piles of beautiful sweet potatoes, carrots, onions and parsnips. I stuck them all in a big roasting pan about three inches deep with plenty of salt and olive oil. When I opened the oven to stir them, a huge cloud of steam greeted me. Nothing was browning or caramelizing, just cooking to mush. They tasted fine and my friends ate them, but I learned one of life's many lessons—some things aren't as simple as they look.

## Two Important Things to Keep in Mind

1) Do not crowd the pan. The veggies will be releasing moisture, and it will evaporate quickly if there is plenty of space. Then the vegetables will get crisp on the outside and soft in the middle. If veggies are crowded together, the moisture won't evaporate quickly enough, and they will steam instead of crisping. They will still be cooked but won't have that delicious caramelized crust.

2) Use separate pans for slow-cooking vegetables. Different root veggies cook at different speeds, so to avoid mushy vegetable syndrome, combine vegetables that cook at the same rate on a pan. Beets and carrots can take a long time to roast. Sweet potatoes and onions roast really quickly. Here are some good pairings:

SLOW: rutabaga, beet, carrot, celeriac
MEDIUM: potato, turnip, radish, parsnip, fennel
FAST: sweet potato, onion, garlic, leek, shallot

## Roast Root Veggies

4 cups diced root vegetables
   (peel veggies with tough outer skin,
   otherwise don't peel)
1 Tablespoon extra virgin olive oil

½ teaspoon salt
Fresh ground pepper to taste
1 Tablespoon chopped fresh herbs

*Preheat oven to 400 degrees. On a large sheet pan, toss together veggies, oil, salt and pepper. Combine vegetables that will cook at the same rate, using a separate pan for slower-cooking veggies. Roast for 15–20 minutes without stirring. Remove pan from the oven and use a metal spatula to stir. Test for doneness by tasting or cutting. Put back in the oven to roast veggies that are not quite done. Stir and test every 5–10 minutes until desired doneness. Sprinkle with fresh herbs and serve hot with an optional glaze or topping on the side.*

### GLAZE AND TOPPING OPTIONS

Root vegetables are beautiful with salt, pepper and fresh herbs, but if you want to get fancy, try sprinkling, drizzling or dipping your veggies in a sauce or glaze.

- Bright-Colored Pepper Sauce (See page 186)
- Honey Balsamic Rosemary Syrup (See page 221)
- Garlic Mustard Butter (See page 98)
- Fresh Herb Remoulade (See page 151)

# Marinated Mustard Dill Potato Salad

SERVES 8

My husband loves the flavors of potato and dill together. When we were young and low on resources, he often made a dish of boiled potatoes dressed with nothing more than fresh dill, plenty of salt and a bit of butter. Those were gloriously simple times, eating meals off of inherited plates, sitting on the front porch steps. Potato and dill will always mean simplicity for me, and this salad reminds me to appreciate all that I have.

10 cups water
8 cups diced potato, unpeeled, 1-inch cubes
2 teaspoons salt

## MARINADE

¼ cup extra virgin olive oil
¼ cup Dijon mustard
¼ cup cider vinegar
4 cloves garlic, very finely diced

4 teaspoons sugar
1 teaspoon salt
2 Tablespoons chopped fresh dill or 1
　　Tablespoon dried

## OPTIONAL

6 cups salad greens
Sliced olives
Sliced hardboiled eggs

Cherry tomatoes
Roasted tomatoes

*Combine water, potatoes and salt in a pot and bring to a boil. Cook until potatoes are just tender, 4–8 minutes. Don't overcook. Meanwhile, mix together marinade ingredients. Drain potatoes and gently combine hot potatoes with marinade. Refrigerate and allow to marinate for 2–3 hours.*

*Serve with salad greens on individual plates, topping with potatoes and optional ingredients. Drizzle marinade on top. Alternatively, serve potato salad without greens as a side dish alongside Green Bean Fritters, pickles, Bacon Apple Beef Burgers, Polenta Tomato Pie, Corn Chow Chow and Smoky Pimento Cheese.*

## Fermented Root Veggies

I got to meet the king of fermentation, Sandor Katz, a few years ago. He has written several books on the subject, and his research shows that fermentation makes foods more nutritious. Winter is the perfect time for a little nutrition boost. Folks who might be leery of funky flavors can control the funk

factor by limiting fermentation time. When veggies taste "funky enough," stick them in the fridge and eat them within a few weeks.

2–4 carrots

3–4 radishes or turnips

Garlic scapes or 2 cloves garlic, peeled

4 wild green onion stalks or 1 shallot or
   small onion, sliced

5–10 black peppercorns

1 teaspoon salt

1 bay leaf

Filtered water

*Wash all vegetables well. Slice carrots and radishes into sticks or rounds and pack into a pint-sized or 2-cup glass jar. Pack all other ingredients into the jar and fill to the top with water so that veggies are completely covered. Put the lid on and shake gently to dissolve salt. Let sit out at room temperature for 3–4 days. The water should be a little bubbly when you open the jar, and the veggies should be softened. Taste veggies—if they are funky enough for you, refrigerate them. If you want a little more flavor, you can leave them out for another day or two. Veggies will keep in the fridge for several months.*

*Add them to salads and tacos or serve as a pickled salad on their own. They are a great thing to take on a picnic for a little crunch.*

# 16

## Winter Squash

I got my picture published in a seed catalogue a few years back because of my neck pumpkins. This variety of squash looks (and tastes) just like a butternut with an incredibly long neck. Often, the neck curls around into a hook that can hang nicely about a person's neck, hence the name. The end of the squash that contains the seeds is tiny in comparison, so processing requires relatively little work for the amount of pumpkin gained.

On our farm, we have a smallish field below our barn where we practice a bit of mono-cropping, meaning that each summer, we plant one variety of vegetable. Generally, I prefer to do companion planting with lots of things growing symbiotically together, but I don't get out to our farm field often enough to care for a complex garden. Planting one variety makes it logistically possible to grow food and has the added benefit of making seed saving possible because plants can't cross-pollinate.

The summer I grew eight hundred pounds of neck pumpkin in our farm field was a good summer. Not only did we get all that delicious pumpkin, but I also got to sell the seeds to a local garden supply company, Sow True Seed, *and* I got my picture in their catalogue.

It took us two years to eat through all the pumpkin I put in the freezer that winter. Equally as good in sweet or savory recipes, I remember at least one dinner party that had neck pumpkin in every single dish, including the gravy.

The following recipes explore the vast variety of ways to consume winter squash. If you happen to have a bumper crop, you can eat squash for breakfast, lunch, dinner and snacks in between. A word of caution, however, from the voice of experience: if your skin starts to turn a bit orange, just skip the squash for a couple of days and you will be back to normal in no time.

# COOKING AND PROCESSING WINTER SQUASH

### ROASTING

I love this method for processing squash because it is relatively hands-off. Once the squash is roasted, it is very easy to remove the skin; the flesh is soft, easy to measure and can even be packed in bags and frozen.

Preheat the oven to 350 degrees. Slice any variety of squash in half and scoop out the seeds. Place on a lightly oiled sheet pan flesh side down. Bake for 45–60 minutes until squash is very soft and skin is blistered. Cool, peel off outer skin and use flesh for any recipe calling for cooked winter squash.

NOTE: If your squash is very very large, check out the technique in the Candy Roaster and Candied Pecan Muffin recipe (page 222) for processing and roasting.

*Author photo.*

### CUTTING, PEELING AND CUBING BUTTERNUT

You can peel and cube just about any winter squash, but some are easier than others. Butternut is one of the easiest because it has thin, smooth skin and a streamlined shape. It can still be intimidating to handle a big squash and a big knife at the same time.

Slice the ends off of the butternut and stand up with the bigger flat end on the cutting board. Make sure squash is nice and stable. (It helps if you are stable too.) Using a large knife, slice butternut in half lengthwise and scoop out the seeds. Using a vegetable peeler, remove skin. Cut into long, one-inch-wide slices, then cut into cubes. Roast with other veggies, steam or braise in liquid on the stove top.

## Thickening Winter Squash Puree

Every squash you cook is going to have a different moisture content depending on the variety and what the weather was like when it was growing. The moisture content can have a dramatic impact on your recipes. Some recipes (especially baked goods) simply will not turn out right if your squash is not the right consistency. Several of the recipes in this book specify thickened winter squash. If the recipe does not specify, then any consistency will work fine.

Roast winter squash and remove skin or cook raw peeled winter squash in a few Tablespoons of water on the stove top in a covered pot until tender. Mash or puree squash and cook in a pot, uncovered, on low heat, stirring occasionally, until consistency of the squash is thick enough so that if you scoop some up in a spoon and turn the spoon upside down squash stays put. This can take up to forty-five minutes depending on how moist your squash is.

### IS ALL WINTER SQUASH THE SAME?

Nope. It's all pretty different actually. But in many cases it can be used interchangeably. A good rule of thumb is that if the flesh is orange it is going to be sweet like butternut, and if the flesh is whitish or yellow, it may not be as sweet. You can definitely substitute one sweet squash for another in all of the recipes in this book. The less sweet winter squashes can also sub in for each other.

Sweet squashes: butternut, pie pumpkins, candy roaster, Cinderella, hubbard, kabocha, delicata
Less sweet (but still awesome) squashes: acorn, spaghetti, pumpkin

## Butternut Spiced Waffles with Honey Balsamic Rosemary Syrup

### SERVES 4

I'm not always a fan of breakfast for dinner—I tend to prefer savory flavors at that time of day—but this sophisticated waffle is an exception. My rosemary plants always need cutting back at about the same time all the winter squash is coming in from the garden, and I can't get enough of that combination. The syrup is equally good on roasted veggies and even salad greens. A little spicy crisp bacon on the side and it starts to look like dinner. Of course, these waffles are good for breakfast, but purists might want maple syrup at that time of day.

## HONEY BALSAMIC ROSEMARY SYRUP

½ cup honey
2 Tablespoons balsamic vinegar
4 (3-inch) sprigs rosemary

## WAFFLES

2 cups all-purpose flour
2 teaspoons baking powder
1 teaspoon salt
1 Tablespoon sugar
1 teaspoon fresh grated nutmeg

1 ½ cups milk
½ cup thick winter squash puree
  (see page 219)
6 Tablespoons butter, melted
2 eggs

*Combine syrup ingredients in a sauce pot and heat on medium until starting to simmer. Remove from heat and let rosemary infuse while you make waffles.*

*Preheat waffle iron to medium heat. Sift together the dry ingredients. Whisk together the milk, squash, butter and eggs. Mix the wet with the dry ingredients. Spoon batter onto waffle iron and spread with a spatula, leaving 1–2 inches around the edges. Grill until brown and crispy. Repeat with remaining batter and keep waffles warm.*

*Remove rosemary sprigs from the syrup. Serve with Honey Balsamic Rosemary Syrup, slices of crisp bacon, roasted veggies, fried chicken, sautéed kale, fig preserves or maple syrup.*

## Candy Roaster and Candied Pecan Muffins

Candy roasters can get really really impressively large, but their flesh stays super sweet. My farmer friend Teresa gave me the secret to processing these somewhat intimidating squash. She said that in her family, they have always taken the big ones out to the patio and dropped them on the concrete. The squash splits into pieces—no big scary knife required. Next, she piles the pieces flesh side down on pans and bakes them. This can be done with any huge winter squash, and you will have enough cooked squash to make zillions of muffins.

NOTE: Canned pumpkin or other sweet winter squash puree can be substituted in this recipe. Makes 12–14 (2-inch) muffins.

## CANDIED PECANS

1½ cups chopped pecans
⅓ cup packed brown sugar
1 Tablespoon water
1 Tablespoon vegetable oil

1 teaspoon vanilla extract
1 teaspoon salt
¼ teaspoon cinnamon

*In a sauce pot, toast the pecans over medium-high heat for 3–4 minutes, stirring often. In a bowl, mix together the other ingredients. Pour over the pecans and quickly mix. Stir constantly for about 1 minute and remove from heat. Set aside and let cool.*

## MUFFINS

2 cups all-purpose flour
1½ teaspoons baking powder
1 teaspoon salt
1½ teaspoons cinnamon
½ teaspoon ginger
¼ teaspoon nutmeg

¾ cup sugar
1½ cups cooked and mashed candy roaster
   or 15 ounces canned pumpkin
⅔ cup milk, soy milk or coconut milk
⅓ cup vegetable oil
1 egg

*Preheat oven to 350 degrees. In a bowl, sift together flour, baking powder, salt and spices. In another bowl, whisk together sugar, squash, milk, oil, egg and about half of the cooled candied pecans. Fold the wet and dry ingredients together until just mixed.*

*Scoop into prepared muffin cups and place remaining candied pecans on tops of muffins. Bake for 25–30 minutes, until toothpick inserted in the center of a muffin comes out clean.*

## Velvety Mac and Cheese

### SERVES 6 (AS A MAIN DISH)

It's not officially winter, but Halloween always seems to be chilly in the mountains, and therefore, it is the perfect time to make a huge batch of mac and cheese. We average about two thousand trick-or-treaters at our house on Halloween, and it takes a village to make sure all those zombies and princesses get a piece of candy when they say the magic words. I invite everyone and anyone over to help, but they have to

be fed something more substantial than candy corn. I make big pans of mac and cheese, garlic bread, veggie platters and dips. By the end of the night, there are candy wrappers everywhere and not a trace of pasta left.

| | |
|---|---|
| 1 pound macaroni or ziti pasta | 2–3 cloves garlic, very finely diced |
| ½ cup milk | 1½ teaspoons salt |
| 1½ cups roasted and pureed butternut, pumpkin or orange-fleshed winter squash | ½ teaspoon Dijon mustard |
| | 1 teaspoon chopped fresh sage (optional) |
| 4 ounces cream cheese, cut in chunks | 1 teaspoon chopped fresh rosemary |
| 4 cups grated sharp Cheddar cheese | (optional) |

In a large pot, bring about 4 quarts of water to a boil. Add pasta to water and cook 8–10 minutes, until pasta is almost, but not quite done. Drain.

Meanwhile, heat milk in a sauce pot. When milk starts to simmer, add in squash and cream cheese, whisk well and add remaining ingredients. Whisk and heat until cheese is melted.

Add drained pasta to cheese sauce and stir well. Depending on the variety of squash, the sauce may be thin. You can continue cooking for several minutes until sauce thickens and the pasta is done. Pour into a 9x13 pan and keep warm in the oven or serve right off the stovetop.

### UPTOWN MAC AND CHEESE

If you are serving a sophisticated crowd, try substituting ¾ cup fresh grated Parmesan, Asiago, aged Gouda or aged provolone cheese for one cup of the Cheddar. You will still have the same velvety consistency but with a richer depth of flavor.

*Author photo.*

## Pan Seared Winter Squash with Cider and Greens

### SERVES 3-4 (AS A SIDE DISH)

The dilemma of what to cook for Friendsgiving parties can be complicated by the fact that you may also have to attend a family Thanksgiving celebration on the same day. God forbid you have multiple family celebrations. Dish after dish of rich creamy casseroles will be passed around the tables, and to avoid offending Aunt Betty, you may be over-served. This light but elegant side dish is the solution. Make it for Friendsgiving or with your weeknight rotisserie chicken. It is good either way.

4 cups peeled, cubed, orange winter squash (1 medium butternut)
1 Tablespoon olive oil
2 shallots (or ½ cup onion), diced
1 teaspoon dried thyme

2 teaspoons Dijon mustard
1 teaspoon salt
3–4 cups mustard, turnip, Swiss chard or kale greens, coarsely chopped
1 cup apple cider (more if needed)

*In a large skillet that you can cover or heavy-bottomed pot, sauté squash in olive oil for about 5 minutes on high. Turn heat down to medium. Add in shallots, thyme, mustard and salt. Stir well to combine and sauté 2–3 more minutes. Top squash with greens—don't stir them in. Add cider to the pan and cover. Cook on medium for 8–10 minutes. Carefully remove lid and sample a bite of squash. If it is still a little hard, cover and cook a few more minutes, adding a bit more cider if needed. Stir to combine greens when squash is done. Serve warm as a side dish with seasoned rice, green bean casserole, mashed potatoes with brown butter, apple chestnut stuffing and roasted or grilled meats.*

# Winter Squash Soup with Green Tomato Sage Croutons

### SERVES 4–6

There is a narrow window when I have green tomatoes at the same time as winter squash. First frost has come and gone, and I've cleaned most things out of the garden. The last green tomatoes sit on the windowsill with a slim chance of turning pink. These tart tomatoes brighten the slightly sweet soup in a way that is hard to imagine until you taste it. It may seem like an awful lot of croutons, but I have found that if you put them in a bowl on the table, people just keep reaching for more.

## SOUP

2 cups diced onion (1 large)
1 teaspoon vegetable or light olive oil
4 cloves garlic, finely diced
8 cups peeled and cubed orange winter
    squash (pie pumpkin, butternut,
    candy roaster, hubbard, kobocha)
    or 6 cups cooked squash

4 cups vegetable or chicken stock
    or water
½ cup heavy cream
1½ teaspoons salt
1 teaspoon hot chili sauce (optional)
Fresh ground pepper to taste

*In a heavy-bottomed stock pot, sauté onion in oil on medium until tender. Add in garlic in the last minute of cooking. Add squash and stock and bring to a boil. Cook for about 10 minutes, covered, or until squash is tender. Add remaining ingredients and puree with a blender or stick blender. Keep soup warm on low until it is served.*

## CROUTON BATTER

1 egg
1 cup finely diced green tomatoes
¾ cup cornmeal
½ cup all-purpose flour
¼ cup buttermilk, milk or soymilk
2 Tablespoons chopped fresh sage
    (or 1 Tablespoon dried)

1 Tablespoon oil
1 teaspoon garlic powder
1 teaspoon salt
2 Tablespoons butter, melted

*Preheat oven to 350 degrees. In a bowl, whisk the egg and add in other ingredients, except melted butter, and mix well. Pour batter into a greased baking pan. Batter should be about ¼ inch thick, spread into an 8-inch square. Bake for 15–20 minutes, until set. Remove from the oven and cut into bite-sized squares. Drizzle with melted butter and toss gently. Return to the oven and bake another 10–15 minutes until crispy and starting to brown. Serve on top of piping hot soup along with Lemon Arugula Apple Salad, Spinach and Sorghum Meatloaf, pot roast, Apple Coleslaw or Potato Mushroom Custard Pie.*

NOTE: If you are making this ahead or serving leftovers, re-toast the croutons before serving.

# WINTER SQUASH DIPS AND SPREADS

I like to host casual gatherings. I do not like to fuss. I'm so impressed when folks individually stuff every endive leaf and lay them on a platter. I am much more likely to stick a bowl of dip in the middle of a platter with endive leaves all around. If presentation is your thing, then these dips will work stuffed in leaves, but if you prefer the no-fuss method, they are pretty in a bowl with dippers on the side. The texture of pureed winter squash is perfect for dip, and the subtle sweetness is nice with cheese and warm winter spices.

## ROASTED RED PEPPER DIP

1 ½ cups cooked winter squash
½ cup roasted red peppers or one large red
   bell pepper, roasted and seeded

2 cloves garlic, crushed and peeled
2 Tablespoons olive oil
1 teaspoon salt

*Puree everything together in a food processor until smooth. Serve with veggies, tortilla chips, crackers or toasted bread.*

## SMOKED CHEDDAR SPREAD

2 cups cooked winter squash
4 ounces (1 cup) smoked Cheddar cheese,
   grated

1 ounce cream cheese
1 clove garlic, crushed and peeled
½ teaspoon salt

*Puree everything together in a food processor until smooth. Serve with apples, crackers and chips or on tacos, BBQ sandwiches and egg sandwiches with pickled onions.*

## BLACK BEAN BUTTERNUT SPREAD

I cup cooked winter squash
I (15-ounce) can black beans, drained
I clove garlic, crushed and peeled
2 Tablespoons olive oil

I teaspoon lemon juice
I teaspoon salt
I teaspoon smoked paprika

*Puree everything together in a food processor until smooth. Serve with tortilla chips or veggie sticks.*

# Mixed Greens with Roasted Butternut and Sorghum Vinaigrette

### SERVES 6

Running with friends while talking about food occurs frequently in my life. I like to work up an appetite, and doing those activities simultaneously means I am highly motivated to cook when I get home. This salad was dreamed up on a trail in the woods, and my mouth watered all the way back to the stove.

## SALAD

8 cups peeled and cubed butternut squash
I teaspoon salt
2 Tablespoons balsamic vinegar
2 Tablespoons sorghum or light molasses

I Tablespoon olive oil
¼ cup rosemary leaves, chopped
6 cups mixed salad greens
I crisp apple, sliced

## SORGHUM VINAIGRETTE

3 Tablespoons balsamic vinegar
2 Tablespoons sorghum or light molasses
2 cloves garlic, finely diced

I Tablespoon olive oil
¼ teaspoon salt

*Preheat oven to 450 degrees. For the salad, combine butternut, salt, vinegar, sorghum and olive oil on a sheet pan. Roast 15–20 minutes until squash is tender. Sprinkle rosemary on top and roast 2–3 more minutes. Allow to cool for 10–15 minutes. Combine vinaigrette ingredients. Put salad greens on serving plates, evenly divide butternut and apple slices between plates and drizzle with dressing. Alternatively, toss all ingredients together in a large bowl just before serving.*

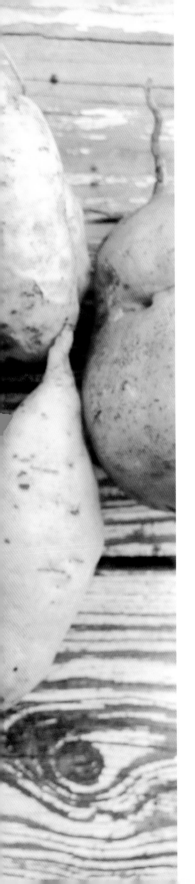

# 17

## Sweet Potatoes

We grow a lot of food in our front yard, and one summer, we grew a ridiculous amount of sweet potatoes. All summer long, as people walked past, they would ask what vine was taking over the sidewalk. When savvy gardeners walked by they would ask what varieties of sweet potatoes we were growing. It was a great neighborhood conversation starter.

Through the summer, we ate sweet potato leaves off the vigorous vines in soups and sautés (see index for recipes), all the while wondering what was happening underground. When September finally came, I could no longer wait. I started digging and found something roughly the size and shape of a football under that first vine.

Well, that was cause for celebration. After showing it off for several days, we fired up the pizza oven and had a pizza party. As the oven was cooling down, we stuck that football-shaped sweet potato in the oven and baked it overnight. Five of us ate our fill of sweet potato for breakfast.

A few weeks later, I pulled the rest of those roots out of the earth in the front yard, filling five bushel baskets with all shapes and sizes of sweet, tasty tubers. This chapter includes many recipes that I developed that fall and winter, which will always be known in my mind as the year of the sweet potato.

# Sweet Potato Salad with Lime and Cilantro

SERVES 8–10

I used to be really involved with the Slow Food movement. It's like the opposite of fast food. We had meetings once a month to plan our activism and fueled our activism with fantastic food. Everyone brought something cooked slowly or prepared with love. I remember tasting wood-fired oven–roasted tomatoes for the first time and couldn't focus on anything else until I had soaked up every drop on my plate with some homemade baguette. If you are looking to fuel some activism, or maybe just some fun, this is a great salad for a meeting or a potluck. Add beans and greens for a main dish salad that will fuel a lot of folks for a good long time.

8 cups (2½ pounds) peeled and
  cubed sweet potatoes
1 red bell pepper, diced
1 green bell pepper, diced
½ cup diced red onion
½ cup loosely packed cilantro leaves,
  chopped
1 lime, finely grated zest, and juice

2–3 cloves garlic, finely diced
2 Tablespoons extra virgin olive oil
1½ teaspoons salt
1 teaspoon sugar (optional)
1 jalapeño pepper, finely diced (optional)
3 cups cooked black beans (optional)
3–4 cups thinly sliced massaged kale or
  sweet potato leaves (optional)

*Bring about 10 cups of water to a boil and add sweet potato cubes. Simmer for about 5–8 minutes and start checking for doneness. When sweet potatoes are tender, but not falling apart, drain them and run cool water over them. Put sweet potatoes in a bowl with remaining ingredients and gently toss to combine. Taste and add sugar or a little more salt if desired. Serve alongside Grilled Peach Salsa, pulled pork tacos, Green Tomato Apple Shallot Salad, Roasted Pepper Hazelnut Rice Salad with Orange and Fig or Spicy Pickled Onions.*

## Sweet Potato Peanut Stew

SERVES 6

In Ghana, cooks don't use cutting boards very often. I have about six cutting boards that I use regularly in my kitchen. So it was very humbling to see cooks expertly peel and slice huge root vegetables with a small paring knife right out of the palm of their hand. I was lost trying to cook in Ghana without my cutting boards. We made stews like this one almost every day, and our kitchen had one cutting board the size of a greeting card. Susie, my Ghanaian cooking teacher, kindly let me use the board because she was scared I would slice off a finger otherwise. Use as many tools and utensils as you want to make this stew, and when you taste it, you might take a moment to appreciate a very long line of cooks cutting up vegetables by any means possible and adding them to the pot.

1 ½ cups diced onion (1 medium)
1 Tablespoon vegetable oil
8 cups (2½ pounds) peeled and cubed
   sweet potatoes
8 cups water
2 cups (about 4 stalks) diced celery
2 cups sliced carrots
2 Tablespoons peeled and
   finely diced ginger

2–3 Tablespoons diced jalapeño peppers
   (2 medium)
4 cloves garlic, very finely diced
1 ½ teaspoons salt
¼ teaspoon cloves
¾ cup peanut butter
3–4 cups cooked white rice for serving
   (see page 185)

### CILANTRO GINGER SAUCE

2–3 cups loosely packed cilantro leaves
   and stems
2 Tablespoons peeled and coarsely
   chopped ginger
½ cup cooked white rice

¼ cup water
2 Tablespoons olive oil
1 Tablespoon lime juice
1 Tablespoon sugar
½ teaspoon salt

*In a large heavy-bottomed pot, sauté onions in oil over medium heat for about 5 minutes or until translucent. Add sweet potatoes and water, bring to a boil and cook covered for about 15 minutes. Sweet potatoes should be tender. Blend mixture with a stick blender or mash thoroughly with a masher. Add in remaining ingredients except rice and peanut butter (nut butter will thicken stew and increase chances of burning on the bottom). Simmer for about 10 minutes until carrots are tender. Add peanut butter and stir until well combined.*

*In a food processor or blender, combine cilantro sauce ingredients and blend for several minutes until very smooth and creamy. Serve stew over rice with cilantro sauce on top.*

## Sweet Potato Biscuits

MAKES ABOUT 8 (2-INCH) BISCUITS

When my friend Kathleen made these biscuits, she was expecting them to taste like sweet potato but was "surprised and excited to find out the sweet potato just made them extra rich and creamy!" She said they were so easy and versatile she was making it her regular biscuit recipe. Maybe it should be everyone's regular biscuit.

*Author photo.*

| | |
|---|---|
| I cup baked, peeled and mashed or pureed sweet potato | 2 teaspoons baking powder |
| ½ cup milk, buttermilk or soy milk | ½ teaspoon baking soda |
| 2 cups all-purpose flour | ½ teaspoon salt |
| | 8 Tablespoons butter |

*Preheat oven to 375 degrees. Whisk together the sweet potato and milk; set aside. In a bowl, combine flour, baking powder, soda and salt. Cut butter into small pieces and work into the flour mixture with fingers until mixture is like a coarse meal (or combine in a food processor). Make a well in the center of the flour and pour the sweet potato mixture in. Mix just until dough forms. If dough seems very dry, add 1–2 Tablespoons more milk.*

*Turn dough out onto floured counter and roll or pat out dough to 1½ inches thick. Use a biscuit cutter (or mason jar lid) to cut biscuits, gather up scraps and repeat. The last bit of dough usually gets twisted together as a yummy baker's treat. Place biscuits on a lightly greased sheet pan and bake 20–25 minutes until golden brown. Serve with honey, jam, eggs, bacon, fried chicken, cheese, soups, salads or just butter.*

### REALLY GOOD BAKED SWEET POTATOES

Some people oil or foil their sweet potatoes before baking, and others cook them in the microwave. Not me. I just stick them on a pan, poke a few holes in the bigger ones and bake them until they are really soft to the touch. Sometimes this takes as long as ninety minutes, and the oven temperature can vary from 325 to 425. Often, if I have the oven on in winter time, it contains a pan of sweet potatoes baking along with whatever bread, casserole, vegetable or pie I turned the oven on to make in the first place. When done this way, the flavor and sweetness concentrates to unbelievable deliciousness, and they are incredibly easy to peel and mash with a fork. The texture and flavor is perfect in biscuits, cornbread, cakes, pies or butterscotch bars. Just as often I'll heat one up and eat it for breakfast because they keep for at least a week in the fridge and I can't resist a little sweetness first thing in the morning.

## Whiskey Braised Sweet Potatoes

SERVES 4–6

Several years ago, I discovered an unfortunate truth: I love whiskey. I prefer some of the dryer Kentucky bourbon–style whiskeys, but really, I like them all. My friend Annie Louise brought over some with sarsaparilla in it that tastes like root beer, and it went down so easily that she forgot to take the rest of the bottle when she left. You won't be forgetting the leftovers of this dish because most of the alcohol gets cooked out of the potatoes, but the wondrous whiskey flavor remains.

¼ cup plus 2–3 Tablespoons whiskey
  or bourbon, divided
1½ cups water
3 Tablespoons butter
2 Tablespoons packed brown sugar
½ teaspoon salt
½ teaspoon chipotle pepper puree
  (optional)

¼ teaspoon ground nutmeg
6 cups (2 pounds) peeled and
  cubed (1-inch) sweet potatoes
1 teaspoon cornstarch
½ cup toasted pecans (optional)

In a wide-bottomed sauce pot, combine ¼ cup whiskey, water, butter, brown sugar, salt, chipotle and nutmeg. Bring to a simmer and add sweet potatoes. Spread potatoes so that they are all at least partially submerged in liquid. Cook uncovered at a low simmer for about 20 minutes. Test a potato to make sure they are cooked through. If they need additional cooking time, cover and simmer 5–10 additional minutes. Mix 2 Tablespoons of whiskey with cornstarch, add to simmering sweet potatoes and stir until thickened. Taste and add additional 1 Tablespoon of whiskey, to taste. Sprinkle with toasted pecans before serving.

Serve as a holiday side dish alongside greens, field peas, corn pudding, Squash Casserole, biscuits, roasted meats, Spinach and Sorghum Meatloaf or Bacon Apple Beef Burgers.

## Sweet Potato Skillet Cornbread

### MAKES ONE CAST-IRON SKILLET FULL

One cold winter evening while sitting in a tiny cabin by the French Broad River with seven wonderful women, I unlocked their secrets to perfect cornbread. My friends and I discussed ancestral family techniques in great detail. If you are from the South, then there are a few things that are consistent about cornbread perfection. It cannot be sweet, and it must be made in some type of cast iron so that it has a delicious crust and moist interior. There is no consensus on the addition of white flour. If you are not from the South, or you have a sweet tooth, then cornbread is typically made with some white flour and enough sugar to taste like cake. The crisp crust is not necessary, but moist interior is still appreciated. Sweet potato is not traditional in either case, but it is my secret to moist, tender cornbread.

¾ cup baked, peeled and mashed or
    pureed sweet potato
2 cups milk, soy milk or buttermilk
2 eggs
¼ cup vegetable oil
2¼ cups cornmeal
2 Tablespoons cornstarch

2 teaspoons baking powder
1 teaspoon salt
¼ teaspoon baking soda
1–2 Tablespoons sugar (optional)
½ teaspoon onion powder (optional)
1 Tablespoon oil or grease for cooking

*Place a 9- or 10-inch oven-proof skillet in the oven and preheat to 375 degrees. In a bowl, whisk together sweet potato, milk, egg and oil. Add remaining ingredients and whisk well. Pull the skillet out of the oven and glaze it with 1 Tablespoon of olive oil, bacon grease or butter. Pour batter into hot pan.*

*Bake for about 25 minutes, until top is golden brown. If you do not have a skillet, make this recipe in any greased 8- or 9-inch pan but increase the baking time about 10 minutes. Serve with butter, honey or jam; alongside soups, salads and chili; or make winter panzanella salad with cubes of toasted cornbread.*

### AVOID THE CRUMBLY CORNBREAD

If you are using stone ground or coarse ground cornmeal, try adding 1–2 Tablespoons additional cornstarch or potato flour to the batter for a texture that does not crumble as much. All-purpose flour is often used in cornbread recipes for this reason, but I prefer the flavor of corn only.

## Sweet Potato Pimento Fritters

MAKES 12–15

These pretty things flecked with red are a solid potluck item. They fulfill my potluck criteria: delicious warm or room temperature, easy to make ahead of time and fits just about any potluck theme. I've served them alongside guacamole, salsa, Indian chutney, pesto, ranch dressing and herb mayo. I haven't tried wasabi and pickled ginger, but it just might work.

2 cups uncooked grated sweet potato
¾ cup diced roasted red peppers or fresh
  pimento pepper
¼ cup grated Parmesan cheese
¼ cup diced onion

2 eggs, whisked
2 teaspoons cornstarch
1 teaspoon salt
½ teaspoon fresh ground black pepper
Oil or grease for frying

*Combine all ingredients in a bowl, except oil or grease. Heat a frying pan or skillet over medium heat and slick with 1–2 teaspoons bacon grease or oil. Scoop 2 Tablespoons of batter at a time into skillet and flatten into fritters with the back of your spoon. Flip after a few minutes and fry until golden brown on both sides. Top fritters with Fresh Herb Remoulade (see page 151), pesto or Cucumber Ranch. Serve warm or at room temperature.*

## *Black Bean Sweet Potato Coconut Soup*

SERVES 4

I remember the first time I had the sweet potato–black bean combination. We were at the beach, and my big sister made a platter of quesadillas with Monterey Jack cheese, chili-spiced black beans and mashed sweet potato. After playing on the beach all day, my stomach was turning inside out with hunger, and I couldn't get enough of the spicy-sweet combination. I still can't get enough of that combination, so I'm always inventing new ways of eating them together.

1 Tablespoon vegetable oil
1 cup diced onion
4 cloves garlic, finely diced
6 cups (2 pounds) peeled and diced
   sweet potatoes
4 cups water
1 (15-ounce) can coconut milk
2 teaspoons chile garlic or Sriracha sauce
1 ¼ teaspoons salt
½ teaspoon cumin
2 (15-ounce) cans black beans

3 cups finely chopped greens (kale, spinach,
   sweet potato greens, bok choy, mustard
   or turnip)
Sliced limes, for serving
Fresh cilantro, for serving

*Heat oil in a heavy-bottomed sauce pot. Add the onion and sauté on medium heat until soft, 5–10 minutes. Add the garlic and sauté 1 more minute. Add all of the remaining ingredients except beans, greens and garnish. Bring to a boil and simmer 10–15 minutes until potatoes are tender. Use a stick blender or blender to puree soup. Add beans and greens and bring back to a simmer. Cook 3–5 minutes until greens are tender. Serve with cornbread, crackers, tortilla chips, toast and a hearty green salad.*

# Sweet Potato Butterscotch Blondies

MAKES 12–16 BARS

I like to spend quite a bit of time with other humans. I know some people are dog people and some people are tree people. I like dogs and trees quite a lot, but I think I am a human person. It's rare that I find a human who can resist the sound of these blondies, and it makes me extremely happy to see them gobbled up.

1 cup baked, peeled and pureed or
  mashed sweet potato
¾ cup sugar
6 Tablespoons butter, melted
⅓ cup milk or soy milk
1 egg
2 teaspoons vanilla extract

1 ¼ cups all-purpose flour
1 teaspoon baking powder
½ teaspoon salt
½ cup butterscotch chips
½ cup semisweet or white chocolate chips
½ cup pecans

*Preheat oven to 350 degrees. In a bowl combine potato, sugar, butter, milk, egg and vanilla. Use a stick blender or whisk to blend. In a separate bowl, sift together flour, baking powder and salt. Fold in the wet ingredients and chips. Do not over mix. Grease an 8x8 square pan and pour the batter in. Sprinkle top with nuts. Bake 35–45 minutes until browning on edges and firm in the middle. Allow to cool before cutting.*

NOTE: For a gluten-free version of this treat, try substituting 1 cup oat flour and ¼ cup coconut flour for the all-purpose flour.

# Chocolate Ginger Sweet Potato Pie

### SERVES 8

I brought this pie to a square dance at a local farm, and I felt like the most popular girl at the dance. I was a bit late, so folks were milling around the checked-clothed buffet table set out in the field. They'd had their fill of kale salad, broccoli pie, pesto pasta and BBQ. Folks were looking for something sweet. I appeared at just the right time with this gorgeous pie, and it was gone within minutes.

## CRUST

4 Tablespoons butter
¾ cup semisweet chocolate chips
1¼ cups graham cracker crumbs

2 Tablespoons sugar
1 teaspoon powdered ginger

## FILLING

2 cups baked, peeled and mashed
  sweet potato
½ cup packed brown sugar
½ cup half-and-half
2 eggs

1 teaspoon powdered ginger
½ teaspoon cinnamon
¼ teaspoon salt
¼ cup chopped crystalized ginger

## TOPPING

3 Tablespoons half-and-half
½ cup semisweet chocolate chips

¼ cup chopped crystalized ginger

*Preheat oven to 350 degrees. For the crust, melt butter in microwave or saucepan. Add chocolate chips and continue to melt, stirring until smooth. Combine with remaining crust ingredients and press into a 9-inch deep-dish pie pan.*

*For the filling, combine all ingredients in a bowl or electric mixer and mix well. Pour filling into crust and bake for 45 minutes to 1 hour. Filling will be starting to brown on edges and will puff slightly in the center.*

*Meanwhile, heat half-and-half for the topping in microwave or saucepan. Add chocolate chips and continue to melt, stirring until smooth. (Note: when melting chocolate, be sure to only use completely dry utensils—water causes chocolate to seize up.)*

*Sprinkle pie with ginger and drizzle with chocolate sauce. Allow to cool at least 15 minutes before serving.*

# Mashed Sweet Potatoes with Decadent Toppings

### SERVES 4

Most folks have experienced a baked potato bar. Everyone gets to dress up their potato with toppings like sautéed mushrooms or chili and cheese. I want to start a new trend with a mashed sweet potato bar, except the toppings would be exotic or decadent and you would try them one at a time. Each of these toppings is excellent and will give you enough choices to keep everyone happy.

## BASIC MASHED SWEET POTATOES

6 cups (2 pounds) peeled and cubed
   sweet potatoes

1 cup water
¼ teaspoon salt

*Combine all ingredients in a pot and bring to a boil. Simmer covered for about 20 minutes until potatoes are quite soft. Use a potato masher or stick blender to mash potatoes. Serve on plates and top with one of the decadent toppings.*

## SMOKED SEA SALT WHIPPED CREAM

½ cup heavy cream
½ teaspoon smoked sea salt

*Use a whisk or electric beaters to whip cream until peaks form. Fold in salt.*

## PARMESAN BEURRE BLANC

¼ cup white wine
¼ cup heavy cream

6 Tablespoons butter
¼ cup freshly grated Parmesan cheese

*Heat wine over moderate heat until reduced by half, about 4–5 minutes. Add cream and bring to a boil. Turn heat to low and whisk in a Tablespoon of butter at a time. Whisk in Parmesan cheese and remove from heat.*

## SORGHUM WHIPPED CREAM

½ cup heavy cream
2 Tablespoons sorghum or light molasses

*Use a whisk or electric beaters to whip cream until peaks form. Whisk in sorghum.*

## WASABI BUTTER

4 Tablespoons butter
1–2 teaspoons wasabi powder

*Soften butter for a few seconds in the microwave or leave out at room temperature for an hour (as long as your room is 70 degrees or more). Stir wasabi into butter to taste.*

# INTERVIEW WITH CHEF VIVIAN HOWARD

If you've seen Vivian Howard's PBS show *A Chef's Life,* you know that she is an amazing cook who draws heavily on her southern upbringing. She is renowned for her delicious renditions of traditional southern dishes at her restaurant Chef and the Farmer in Kinston, North Carolina, and in her beautiful book *Deep Run Roots: Stories and Recipes from My Corner of the South.* What you may not know about Vivian is that she came to cooking by way of writing.

Living in New York City and aspiring to write about food meant that Vivian worked in restaurants "to get a behind-the-scenes look at what was really going on." She found that she loved the cooking, camaraderie, teamwork and, most importantly, found she was good at these things.

Working as a server at Voyage, a restaurant in Greenwich Village with a menu built around the concept of southern food via Africa, Vivian was fascinated by the stories of how the slave trade affected our foodways in the South. "I latched on to the food and food storytelling because it was about my place, but I was really interested in learning about other places."

After learning about all kinds of other cuisines, Vivian came back to the "farmer's food" that she grew up eating when she opened her restaurant in Kinston. Drawing inspiration from the limitations that farmers used to have when they cooked, Vivian works with fresh, seasonal produce. "I try to work with a limited pantry based on what people grow here. My creative process is based on preserving abundance for lean times." This means pickling, fermenting and preserving the harvest so she can serve blueberries in February.

Vivian's goal is to always have a plan for something when she preserves it. At the restaurant, they have standbys like watermelon rind pickles that they make each year, but experimenting with adding spices like star anise and cloves keeps things interesting. She stresses, however, that "sometimes it makes more sense to keep your pickle or preserve simple so that you can add to or tweak it later and use it in a variety of applications."

Living where she does, Vivian ends up canning a lot of tomatoes and always has them on hand. Having home-canned tomatoes in your pantry is like money in the bank, she says, since there are so many delicious possibilities. Vivian's favorite is to braise greens with the tomatoes, add herbs and eat them with beans. Simple, traditional and soul-satisfying.

## Vivian's Sweet Potato Wedges with Tahini and Sesame

| | |
|---|---|
| 1 sweet potato, cut into 8–10 thick wedges | 1 lemon, juiced |
| 1 Tablespoon extra virgin olive oil | 1 teaspoon toasted sesame oil |
| 3 Tablespoons tahini | ⅛ teaspoon salt |
| 3 Tablespoons honey | |

*Preheat the oven to 400. In a mixing bowl, coat the sweet potato wedges in extra virgin olive oil and a liberal sprinkling of salt. Arrange them on a baking sheet with the flesh side down. You will need to flip the wedges once, halfway through the cooking process. Place the baking sheet on the middle rack of the oven and bake for 50–60 minutes. Keep an eye on the potatoes as they cook; you are looking for a gold-brown, crispy exterior and a softer, creamier interior.*

*In a separate mixing bowl, whisk together the tahini, honey, lemon juice, sesame oil and salt. When the potatoes are done, put them on a serving plate and drizzle them with the tahini mixture. Optional garnishes that would be good for this dish are fresh cilantro, sliced scallion and sesame seeds.*

# Index

# About the Author

Cathy Cleary and her husband, Reid Chapman, moved to West Asheville, North Carolina, in 1995. Cathy and her business partner Krista Stearns opened the West End Bakery Café in 2000. She devoted her heart and soul to this iconic establishment until they sold the business in 2015.

Cathy began cooking and baking at the ripe age of four and, under her father's tutelage, learned to scrape the mixing bowl clean and use up every scrap of food, never wasting a drop. He taught her scratch-made techniques using whatever ingredients were on hand. She employs these methods today in her professional and home cooking and encourages others to do the same.

She published her first cookbook, *The West End Bakery and Café Cookbook*, in 2014 and was featured as a contributor in *The Carolina Table* by Eno Publishers in 2016. She is ever curious about new preparation techniques and shares her recipes and ideas on her website, The Cook and the Garden.

Food justice, sustainable agriculture, food security and edible education are issues Cathy passionately supports. In 2009, she co-founded a nonprofit called FEAST that teaches gardening and cooking education to over 1,100 kids in schools and afterschool programs in Asheville and Buncombe County. She volunteers with FEAST to envision and enable a community where kids eat vegetables every day regardless of income level. In other volunteer work, Cathy has served on boards of directors such as Bountiful Cities, Slow Food Asheville, Carolina Ground, Haywood Road Market Co-op and AB Tech Culinary Advisory Committee.

Cathy and Reid own a small farm outside of Asheville where they are humbled to realize on a regular basis that growing food is a privilege. By purchasing this book, you are supporting work in the areas of food justice, sustainable agriculture and edible education. To find out how you can do more, send Cathy a message through her website cathycleary.com or thecookandgarden.com.